D1240885

James C. "Jim" Warren began his military career as one of the original Tuskegee Airmen, entering the Army Air Forces in March 1943, and retiring 35 years later as Lieutenant Colonel in November 1978. He served in World War Two with the 477th Bombardment Group (Medium), and flew more than 173 combat missions in the Korean and Vietnam wars. He received numerous awards for his service, including the Distinguished Flying Cross with two Oak Leaf Clusters, the Air Medal with 11 Oak Leaf Clusters, three Meritorious Service Medals, the Air Force Commendation Medal, and several other citations.

His flying career of more than 12,000 hours was highlighted by being selected as the navigator of *Homecoming One*—the first C-141 to fly into Gia Lam, North Vietnam, to return the first group of American POWs to Clark Air Force Base in the Philippines. He was also part of the Apollo 14 recovery team—flying the Apollo crew from splashdown near Pago Pago, American Samoa, to the Manned Space Center at Houston, and flying the Bob Hope Christmas Show on segments of their Southeast Asia tour in 1964.

Jim graduated from the University of Nebraska, and is a life member of Kappa Alpha Psi, and of the Tuskegee Airmen, Inc. After retiring from the Air Force, he worked as a personnel specialist for General Dynamics Corporation. He resides with his wife, Xanthia, in Vacaville, California.

THE
FREEMAN FIELD
MUTINY

By James C. Warren
Lt. Col., USAF (ret)

To Michael [handwritten inscription]

The Conyers Publishing Co
1996

Second printing 1995

Third Printing 1996

Fourth Printing 1997

Published by The Conyers Publishing Company
1242 Hidden Oaks Court, Vacaville CA 95687

Cover and book design by K. O. Eckland

Library of Congress Cataloging-in-Publication Data
Warren, James C.
    The Tuskegee Airmen Mutiny at Freeman Field
    by James C. Warren, Lt. Col. USAF (ret)
        P. cm
        including bibliographical references and index

        TXu 589 178
        Printed in the United States of America

ISBN Number 0-9660818-C-3

Contents

Foreword

Because many of us were extremely concerned, actively involved, or striving to become a part of the American dream, we remember vividly the social revolutions of the '60s. The racial struggles of the '40s were equally important, but too often are remembered only by those who actually served to right the social injustices of that period. Indeed, that era in American history is frequently but a blur to those who have only heard stories relating to the social conditions of America just prior to and during World War Two.

This book is a careful account of a truly history-making event from that dim period that now seems so long ago. The book is the long-awaited story of a mutiny against social injustices by black officers in the United States Army Air Corps during World War Two. In the style of the tribal storyteller, the men involved in this mutiny have for a half-century told, retold, and listened to each other recount the events that led to the incident.

This detailed story of the mutiny is told by Lt. Col. James C. Warren, an original Tuskegee Airman, and an active participant in the mutiny itself. In this significant work he explores what it meant to be a Negro in the United States Army Air Forces during World War Two, and to have been a part of the first stirring of the social revolution in the military.

The United States military establishment has partly, though not entirely, been forced to readjust its traditional social fabrication of race, and to realize that the old way was stupid, morally wrong, and insupportable by scientific facts. The United States should feel indebted to Jim Warren for his candor in addressing this fundamental issue. We were not the first and we will not be the last who did what was necessary for our heritage and, no less, for our pride.

William B. Ellis, Fighter Pilot,
Co-founder and Past President,
Los Angeles Chapter, Tuskegee Airmen

Introduction

The Freeman Field Mutiny was much more than a chance occurrence. It was more than some irrelevant historical curiosity. In no way can it be considered merely a sudden, haphazard response to an isolated set of circumstances. Although the focus of the mutiny was an Army Air Force officers club that refused to admit black officers, including combat veterans, those of us who participated in the mutiny knew that higher stakes were involved.

The mutiny was one battle in the continuing struggle against discrimination and the institutionalized segregation in the armed forces of the United States in 1945. It is important to remember that other battles for acceptance, if not equality, were being fought continuously in all branches of the service, at all levels.

The more significant struggles, certainly those with the highest visibility, occurred in the Army Air Forces during World War Two. The explanation lies in the fact that only in the Air Forces was there an appreciable number of officers, mostly young, able, well-educated, and militant—militant for that era, in any event.

During World War Two, the Armed Services of the United States was severely discriminatory, and all units of the services were segregated. The government and the War Department had maintained an exclusion policy just as it had in all of the country's previous wars.

However, since the end of World War One, organizations within the black community have persevered and exerted pressure upon the War Department to change these policies.

In the fall of 1940, the black community confronted the War Department and demanded full participation in the military service, and employment in the war industry. Such men as Walter White, A. Philip Randolph, Roy Wilkins, Charles Hill, Robert Vann, and Arnold Hill were at the forefront of the movement.

A. Philip Randolph was the quintessential black leader during this period. He was the president of the Brotherhood of Sleeping Car Porters, the only black union in the American Federation of Labor. He remembered what had happened after World War One. Blacks had volunteered to serve in a segregated army for a segregated government, confident that after the war their sacrifices would be rewarded. When black veterans returned in 1919, they got a nice parade through Harlem and little else—no jobs, no challenges to segregation, no progress. Therefore, Randolph and others were determined that the same thing would not happen again. And the time to ensure that, he believed, was at the beginning of the war, not at the end.

In the spring of 1941, Randolph went to the White House with what he called a proposal, but what was, in President Roosevelt's eyes, at least, really a threat. In the booming voice of the opera singer he had once been, Randolph said there had to be a fair employment practice commission, with the power to investigate discrimination in government agencies and in companies working under government contracts in order to ensure equal employment opportunities for blacks in both. He realized that obtaining congressional approval of such a measure would be difficult. However, it would be possible for the President to create a temporary committee by executive order. To demonstrate the importance of this demand, he said he would bring a hundred thousand blacks to Washington on July 1, 1941, for a massive protest march.

It was within the context of the resulting Fair Employment Practice Commission that Randolph included the most important demand that was to affect blacks in aviation. The demand was for the immediate designation of centers where Negroes would be trained for work in all branches of the aviation corps. He said it was not enough alone to train pilots. In addition, navigators, bombardiers, gunners, radiomen, and mechanics must be trained in order to facilitate full Negro participation in the air service.

The President then sent his wife and Fiorello LaGuardia, the mayor of New York City, to visit Randoph at his union headquarters to try again to persuade him to change his mind. They did their best. They told Randolph that Washington's police force was filled with white Southerners who could not be trusted to protect the marchers. There was danger of violence. "There's going to be bloodshed and death in Washington... You're going to get Negroes slaughtered," LaGuardia told him. "If you bring a hundred thousand people there," Eleanor Roosevelt added, "nobody will be able to control them."

Randolph was undeterred. Blacks were already serving in the armed services, he argued, and they had earned a right for full participation, and to jobs in war plants, as well. "But they won't get employed by merely wishing for it." And so LaGuardia and Mrs. Roosevelt left, and Randolph went back to work.

President Roosevelt was in a quandary. He did not want a march, but he did not want an employment commission either. Southerners in Congress were already opposing him on almost everything he tried to do, and even whispering the idea that a fair-employment rule would set them off like Roman candles. In the House of Representatives, John Rankin of Mississippi had already made 16 speeches denouncing the idea, each more vituperative than the last.

Representative Arthur Miller of Nebraska had called Randolph "the most dangerous Negro in America." Theodore Bilbo, the infamous race-baiting Senator from Mississippi, was nearly apoplectic every time the idea was mentioned. Besides, Roosevelt argued, if he issued a fair-employment order for Negroes, who else would be next? He told Randolph at another White House meeting, this time before the entire cabinet, "It would help the Germans."

Randolph refused to yield, and Roosevelt finally had to make a choice: a march or a commission. He chose the commission. The President sent a message to a young lawyer on his staff, Joseph L. Rauh, Jr.: "We need an Executive Order for a Fair Employment Practices Commission, and we need it in a few hours." It became the famous Executive Order 8802—the first of many to deal with racial discrimination. It included a phrase, coined by Rauh as he worked hastily against his deadline, that was to become one of the most powerful and familiar in American life: "No discrimination on grounds of race, color, creed, or national origin."

Randolph cancelled the march.[1]

As a result of relentless pressures by black leaders, culminating in their demand for a fair employment practices commission just before World War Two, young blacks were finally accepted into the Army Air Corps. However, their participation was limited to training as fighter pilots. This severe limitation met only a part of the demands.

The War Department very reluctantly agreed to form a medium bombardment group equipped with the B-25J— the 477th Bombardment Group (M). This decision required the training of black multi-engine pilots as well as navigators, bombardiers, gunners, and radiomen, and jarred the Air Forces throughout.

The 477th Bombardment Group was activated on January 15, 1944, without a backlog of trained personnel. All the key officers were white—most did not care about the needs of the unit. This organization was crippled from the outset. It was subverted by the very persons charged with its success. At the beginning, the morale of the group was at once high, fragile, and sensitive, but its bearing, uniform, marching, and saluting, all superficial symptoms, were as correct and smart as any unit in First Air Force.

This is a story about a mutiny in the 477th that occurred at Freeman Field, Seymour, Indiana, in April 1945. The incident involved 104 black officers. This story covers the period of activities within this group from March 1, 1945, through July 31, 1945.

The sordid history of acts of segregation committed by the commanders of the Black 477th Bombardment Group is long and involves many separate incidents. Yet the Freeman Field Mutiny is the most vivid and outstanding response of them all, effecting a huge change in the 477th Bombardment Group. It is remarkable that Maj. Gen. Frank O.D. (Monk) Hunter, the antagonist, could have pursued his policy of segregation for over 18 months without serious opposition. Conduct of this nature could only have taken place with compliance of commanders and staff persons at Army Air Forces Headquarters level. This undoubtedly included Gen. Henry H. "Hap" Arnold, Commanding General of the U. S. Army Air Forces, and consequently every level of his command and staff.

The young black officers who mutinied were thoroughly fed up with segregation. While looking forward to a permanent career in civilian life after the war, the black officer was quite willing to risk his temporary military career by attacking racial discrimination. The kind of man selected to become a pilot—an officer, and a leader of men—was highly unlikely to submit to what they knew was a clearly illegal policy.[2]

The Freeman Field Mutiny was a protest, and an assault on the segregated policies of Gen. Hunter and the Air Staff at Headquarters Army Air Forces. The mutiny illustrated that the black officer was capable of showing initiative and anger. Moreover, he could also organize and use regulations to his advantage. This action was unprecedented in the annals of the Army Air Forces.

Those of us who followed our conscience and stood together at Freeman Field that fateful day have some confidence that our actions helped make necessary, even inevitable, the significant changes that would soon come.

Many of us who cheered President Truman's executive order ending segregation in the Armed Forces in 1948, just three years later, could not help but feel justified in the risks we had taken, and the sacrifices we had made.

James C. Warren, Lt. Col. USAF (ret)

Acknowledgments

I began this book in June of 1992. Since then, many dedicated people have been of help to me. First, I must give profound thanks to Mrs. Vivian M. White, formerly the research person at the United States Air Force's Museum; she insisted that this was a book I must write. I gratefully acknowledge the assistance of Mrs. Barbara Grenquist, who so patiently guided me through the early days of manuscript preparation. She gave me helpful comments that set me on the correct path. The help I received from Mrs. Linda Yancy was superb. When she read this manuscript, she gave an immense attention to details and offered a list of suggestions that made a great difference. Mrs. Pat Anthony also read the manuscript and gave me encouragement. Mr. William "Wild Bill" Ellis, with his encouragement and good humor shared during many late-night telephone conversations, hiked my spirits, and gave my ebbing enthusiasm a boost. I acknowledge the assistance of J. Alfred Phelps, the author of *Chappie*. I owe a special debt to Dr. Alan L. Gropman, author of *The Air Force Integrates*. It was through his hard work that the information upon which this story is based was unclassified and made available. In addition, he shared his vast knowledge of the subject unselfishly. Donna Ewald published it. She put me in the capable hands of a fine editor, James R. Soladay, who did a superb job. I am pleased to acknowledge the help that came from Mrs. Mary B. Dennis, Deputy Clerk of the Court, Department of the Army Judiciary and Mr. Calvin Jefferson of the National Archives. Special thanks to my friend Mr. Lerone Bennet Jr., of *Ebony*. In his letter he urged me to "Keep on keeping on." And finally, a much deserved acknowledgment to my wife Xanthia, for her support every step of the way.

1

The Mutiny Begins

It was almost dusk on the 3rd of April, 1945, just two days before the last of us would be moving to Freeman Field. We were the replacement group, the final group of black officers in the 477th Bombardment Group left at Godman Field. Ten of us were gathered around a lone B-25 parked on the ramp outside of the operations building at Godman. We were intently listening to Lt. William "Wild Bill" Ellis, who had just landed on a reassignment flight from Freeman Field.

Bill had been identified by Col. Robert R. Selway, Commander of the 477th Bombardment Group, as an agitator and had been kicked out of Freeman Field. He was being sent back to Godman even though he was one of the more senior pilots in both flying time and graduation date. Bill was one of the more mature officers in the group and was willing to spend a lot of time with the younger officers sharing his experience.

Many of us younger officers looked up to "Wild Bill" as a role model. He was a gregarious officer with a quick wit, and, most of all, he was respected for his straightforward personality no less than his flying skills. He was a natural leader. He was one of the taller pilots, 6'-1", trained as a fighter pilot, but upon the formation of the bomber group he had been switched over to the bombers. He was describing the situation at Freeman Field. If anyone could explain the situation at Freeman in a calm and precise manner, it would be Bill. He had our undivided attention. At that moment we were more interested in what he was saying about the officers clubs at Freeman than we were in the flying conditions and the operational flying that may have been going on at Freeman.

At Godman, supported by Bill's additional information, the word had spread about the insufferable club arrangement at Freeman Field. Several of us had read a copy of the new letter order dated April 1, 1945, which confirmed the official plan for deepening the segregation within the group, and we were extremely angry. Bill ran down the details of how Col. Selway had set up two officers clubs, how he had designated the main Officers Club as Officers Club Number Two and restricted its use to the white officers or instructor-supervisors, how he had designated the former white Non-Commissioned Officers Club as Officers Club Number One for use by the black officers or trainees, how this club was promptly dubbed "Uncle Tom's Cabin," and was not used by the black officers. However, Bill pointed out that the black officers there "are not doing a hell of a lot about the other club, Officers Club Number Two. They do not have a plan for fighting this arrangement with enough vigor," said Bill.[3]

We greeted this news with dismay and disgust, and felt an overpowering need to take more substantial action to combat this insulting arrangement. This news heightened our anger, and we vowed to take concrete steps once we arrived at Freeman.

We had just received the news that the 332nd Fighter Group was setting records in Europe, shooting down 25 enemy planes on March 31 and April 1, 1945. It was time that we displayed equal courage and carried on the fight for equality here at home in the 477th. We were convinced that a showdown situation was necessary to resolve this club problem. The black officers of the replacement unit took the initiative.

That evening, under the guidance of Lt. Coleman A. Young, a meeting was held to develop a plan of action to deal with this situation immediately upon arrival at Freeman Field. We were not in a mood to wait longer as we could not see that the situation would improve without action. Coleman was a more mature officer who had received his commission from Infantry Officers Training School at Fort Benning, Georgia. He was a natural leader who had earned his wings the hard way. He had been eliminated from pilot training, but went on to graduate from bombardier school. He had been a primary leader in our protest at Midland Army Air Field, Texas, a protest that involved black officers and a base officers club—a protest similar in nature to our present situation. Through creative negotiation we had won our battle there and had been allowed to become members of the Officers Club at Midland Army Air Field without a protracted fight. Moreover, Lt. Young was experienced in protesting unfair treatment, as he had been active in union organizing in Detroit before entering the service. There he had earned the nickname "Detroit Red."

The Plan

During this first meeting there was no blustering rhetoric, merely a calm discussion of the situation. We were looking for some method of resolution that would solve the conflict without compromising our right of equal and fair treatment as officers in the United States Army Air Forces.

A military environment provided no clear avenue for conflict resolution, especially between the higher and lower ranks and, more conspicuously, between the black officers and the all-white power structure. Furthermore, we wanted to employ some form of creative negotiation. We knew there was no reason to expect any cooperation from Maj. Gen. Frank O.D. (Monk) Hunter, Commanding General of the First Air Force, or Col. Selway. Hunter had already demonstrated his approach to managing any conflict between himself and the black officers of the 477th Bombardment Group. He had mandated that there was no segregation or discrimination within the group; yet, contradictorily, had made clear that there would be no mixing of the races in the Officers Club at Freeman Field.

As our meeting progressed, and suggestions of various courses of action began to surface, the proceedings became very heated. Not everyone there believed that radical action was necessary or should be adopted to protest this order. For instance, a senior medical officer spoke up, "Fellows, I don't think you are going about this in the right way. There is a base regulation out, and you have to obey a base regulation." He added several more comments objecting to our tentative plan. Almost immediately 2nd Lt. Leonard A. Altemus, a tall and athletically-built young officer, threatened to throw him out of the meeting bodily. In fact, Altemus had the good Captain by the seat of his pants and was headed toward the nearest window. Cooler heads prevailed and the officer was allowed to leave the meeting under his own power. Nevertheless, this action sent a message to all of us involved that this was serious business. We had come a long way in the fight to be a part of army aviation and must not let up in that fight. We were serious, and felt an overpowering need to take action and not accept this type of treatment. We saw our problem as a deep-rooted and bitter conflict, and that we were involved in a non-negotiable confrontation. Any negotiated settlement was out of the question. The group settled down and began to finalize the action plan.

MAIN BRANCH
301 N. ELM STREET
TUSKEGEE, AL 36083
TELEPHONE (334) 727-2560

MONTGOMERY WEST
100 COMMERCE STREET
MONTGOMERY, AL 36104
TELEPHONE (334) 262-0800

MONTGOMERY PROMENADE
2774 EAST BOULEVARD
MONTGOMERY, AL 36117
TELEPHONE (334) 277-7001

Deposits made on Saturday are treated as being received on the next business day.

09/07/02 11:40:14 TELLER: 0032
SEQ: 033 ACCOUNT: 0216014500
TRAN AMOUNT: 198.00
BALANCE: 695.47
DDA REGULAR DEPOSIT

FIRST
TUSKEGEE
BANK
MEMBER FDIC

Col. Selway had refused to discuss the problem since the 477th had moved to Freeman Field, denying that segregation existed in the management of the clubs. His denial removed the option of solving the problem by discussion and left us only direct confrontation. The resulting plan, as with all great plans, was elegantly simple: "Go to the Club."

Action

In the early morning hours of April 5, 1945, at a railroad siding of the huge Fort Knox Army Base adjacent to Godman Field, the remaining members of the Combat Crew Training Squadron of the 477th Bomber Group boarded a troop train for Freeman Field, Indiana. The train would arrive at Freeman Field at approximately 4:45 in the afternoon. Our plan was that upon arrival at the base, each officer would go to his assigned quarters, settle in, and immediately go and have dinner. Soon after dinner we would all go to the white-only Officers Club Number Two and request service. We would go in small groups of not more than five officers at a time. We planned close enough intervals to be supportive, yet not to appear as a mass coordinated group.

We anticipated that any black group of officers entering that Club would meet some resistance. We assumed that Col. Selway would react immediately with severe counter-measures, including, possibly, arrest. If arrested, we would conduct ourselves in such a manner as not to create a distasteful situation. Specifically, we were determined to display our strict discipline and prevent any untoward event from occurring.

Some previous accounts of this incident have indicated that we sought to avoid arrest. Yet we knew if Selway insisted on black officers not being served and not being allowed to use that Club, and we entered the Club anyway, there would be a high probability that we would be arrested. Consequently, we had discussed what to do if arrested. If arrested, we would immediately leave the Club, and would not commit any acts of violence or otherwise act in any manner that would diminish or be destructive to our primary goal. This was a non-violent protest. We would do everything "by the book." Likewise, we would continue to enter the club in small groups, as long as the Club remained open for business.

Arrested!

Following the evening meal three black officers, Lt. Robert Payton, Lt. Clifford Garrett and F/O Marcus Clarkson, went to the Club and were told they would not be admitted. Lt. Payton questioned the Club Officer, Maj. Andrew M. White, as to the reason they were not being admitted. White told Payton, "Let's be frank with one another. The truth of the matter is that colored officers aren't allowed in this Club, whether you are base personnel or not." This group left the Club, and, on their way back to the BOQ, they met a larger group of officers and turned around to return to the Club.

I was in that larger group. As I approached that luxurious Officers Club at Freeman Army Air Field, Seymour, Indiana, it occurred to me that we were not an ordinary group of officers going to the Officers Club for an evening of relaxation. No, we were on a well-planned and well-briefed mission. We were determined that flagrant segregation and discrimination would not go uncontested. We were taking a giant step along the road toward the dignity desired and deserved by this group. This trip to the Club was of such importance that each of us had taken special care to ensure that we were in compliance with every sentence in the dress code for officers. We had been carefully briefed on the replies to give to certain questions. We did not want any other issues to dilute the purpose of our mission.

We were walking in groups of four or five; yet, within the group there was very little conversation. My thoughts probably reflected the thoughts of others in the group. I knew that our mission was unusual and fraught with danger, but this was the path we had chosen, and we were acting as a force of light against the forces of darkness. We were a group of young, hot-blooded, black men concentrated on one base, reinforcing in one another the ideals and ambition that brought us here, the first of our kind, into United States Army aviation. It never crossed my mind that we could be making history.

We were all very young. The average age was approximately 21. I was approaching my 22nd birthday in August of that year. We were excited, and at the same time apprehensive. We were about to challenge the power structure of the Army Air Forces in time of war. I looked back at my quarters and realized it was too late to have second thoughts. Whatever happened tonight, things would never be the same.

What we did not know is that at approximately 7 p.m., on April 5, 1945, Maj. Joseph A. Murphy, commanding "C" Squadron, 118th AAF Base Unit, received a surreptitious telephone call from a black officer. The caller advised him that a number of newly-arrived officers from Godman Field had made plans to go to the base Officers Club that night and demand that they be allowed to enter and enjoy the privileges of the Club. Maj. Murphy immediately called Col. Selway and conveyed this information. Selway called Maj. Baumgardner, the Post Provost Marshal, and ordered him to station the Assistant Provost Marshal at the door of the Club specifically for the purpose of enforcing the provisions of a letter order dated April 1, 1945. Selway also called Maj. A. M. White, the officer in charge of Officers Club and Mess Number Two and ordered him to lock all of the Club doors, except the front door.

The entrance into the Club contained a small porch with double wooden and screen doors, lighted by a single, overhead; naked light bulb. That night, in the doorway stood a single white officer dressed in full uniform. He was wearing on his hip, in a webbed holster, the standard Army issue .45-caliber automatic weapon. On his left arm a brassard indicated that his duty that night was the Officer of the Day.

It is important to keep in mind that the Officer of the Day represents the Commanding Officer, and acts for him and the Base Provost Marshal. On April 5, the Officer of the Day was 1st Lt. J. D. Rogers. It was no accident that he was at that place at that time. He was there to perform a single duty. Lt. Rogers' sole responsibility that night was to bar the entry of any black officers who would try to enter the Club, and he was about to go to work, for he had spotted the first group of approaching officers.

Why were we to be stopped from entering the Club? Why were we not to be allowed in this Club? Simply because we were black. Lt. Rogers was determined to prevent us from entering, and we were just as resolved to enter the Club.

The first officer to enter was Lt. Marsden A. Thompson. He was about two paces into the Club when he was met by Lt. Rogers. Rogers said, "This Club isn't for you fellows." Lt. Thompson asked, "Why isn't it for us fellows?" At this time Rogers asked Thompson to step outside the door to continue their conversation. Most us had arrived at the entry at about the same time and stopped to listen to the discussion. Rogers said, "It is a base Officers Club and is for the use of base officers only." Lt. Shirley Clinton, who was standing nearby, spoke up stating that he was a base officer. He asked, "Why am I not allowed to go in the Club?" Rogers answered, "I can't answer that." When Lt. Thompson turned and entered the Club, Rogers followed and grabbed Thompson by the arm. I heard Thompson tell Rogers to take his hands off him. With the rest of the group, I proceeded into the Club. Some conversation continued between Rogers and Clinton. Thompson proceeded toward the telephone, and I approached the bar and ordered a beer. The bartender, a black enlisted person stared at me in disbelief and did not know what to do. Other black officers were also attempting to get service, but the bartender simply did not move. Some of the officers walked over to the pinball machines and began to play.

Maj. Andrew M. White, the Club Officer, appeared, and began beckoning to all of the group to come near him. He was standing in the doorway that was the entrance to the bar. After all the officers were assembled there, White said, "If you men refuse to leave, I will have to place you under arrest." Lt. Thompson said to White, "Major, Sir, we are not refusing to leave, but would like to know why we must leave." White replied, "I have orders." He then took everyone's name, after which he stated, "You are placed under arrest in quarters." We all left the Club.

The following is a list, in the order that our names were taken, of the first 19 officers who entered the Club:

Marsden A. Thompson, 2nd Lt
Robert S. Payton Jr., 2nd Lt
Roland A. Webber, F/O
Coleman A. Young, 2nd Lt.
Davis J. Brown, 2nd Lt.
Leonard E. Williams, 2nd Lt.
Robert L. Hunter, 2nd Lt.
Clifford C. Jarrett, 2nd Lt.
Cyril P. Dyer, 2nd Lt.

Marcus E. Clarkson, F/O
Frank V. Pivalo, F/O
Shirley R. Clinton, 2nd Lt.
Lester B. Norris, 2nd Lt.
Howard Storey, F/O
Clifton Barnett, 2nd Lt.
Charles R. Taylor, F/O
Edward R. Tabbanor, F/O
Norman A. Holmes, F/O
James C. Warren, F/O

Lt. Rogers and Maj. White returned to the bar, probably thinking they had handled a small incident very well. They hardly had a chance to relax when, according to plan, 14 additional black officers entered the Club. White was forced to repeat his last scenario. White listed the names, and placed this group of officers under arrest. He was joined by Capt. Anthony Chiappe, Commander of the 118th Base Squadron (CCTS), who said he wanted to see all the men when White got through with them. When the men were assembled with Capt. Chiappe, he stated that if we had any grievances, we should take them up with him in the morning, that he was the Commanding Officer and he would see what he could do about it. He ended his comments with the order, "You men go to your barracks."

Again the arrested officers departed the Club, and I am sure this time the duty officers thought it was over for the night. Yet as Lt. Rogers went to the door, he observed three other questionable officers entering the Club. The officers were 2nd Lt. James V. Kennedy, 2nd Lt. Roger C. Terry and F/O Oliver Goodall. Rogers had a problem when the officers came closer. He was not sure that they were three black officers—Terry and Kennedy had all the characteristics of whites, though there was no doubt about Goodall. Rogers pressed on and confronted these officers, and attempted to bodily prevent one of the officers, Roger C. Terry, from entering the Club. He later claimed that Terry shoved him aside to enter the Club. Maj. White arrested these three officers. In the meantime, Maj. Baumgardner had arrived at the Club in time to refuse admittance to three other black officers who had attempted to enter. These officers departed without incident or arrest. White then closed the Club for the night. A total of 36 black officers had been arrested that night.

The following day, Col. Selway was confident that the officers arrested the night before represented the sole group of agitators, and he reopened the Club without a Provost Marshal on duty at the door. Delighted, we continued to implement our plan. At 1515 hours, the following officers entered the Club:

> Robert O'Neal, 1st Lt.
> William H. Johnson, 1st Lt.
> Herbert A. Harris, 1st Lt.
> S. W. Green, 1st Lt.
> C.E. Lewis, 2nd Lt.
> Leonard A. Altemus, 2nd Lt.
> Frank B. Sanders, 2nd Lt.
> George W. Prieleau, 2nd Lt.
> Edward W. Watkins, 2nd Lt.
> C. Williams, F/O
> Maurice J. Jackson, F/O
> C. F. Lawrence, F/O
> D. J. Murphy, F/O
> Sidney H. Marzette, F/O
> A. B. Steele, F/O
> Harry S. Lum, F/O
> W. H. Miller, F/O

At 1520 hours:

> Edward V. Hipps, 2nd Lt

At 1540 hours:

> William B. Ellis, 1st Lt
> Spann Watson, 1st Lt.
> Le Roy F. Gillead, 2nd Lt.
> P. T. Anderson, F/O
> Harry R. Dickerson, F/O

At 1545 hours:

> Arthur B. Polite, 1st Lt.
> James W. Mason, 2nd Lt.

No effort was made to prevent these officers from entering. However, Maj. White intercepted each group of officers, took their names, placed them under arrest in quarters, and ordered them from the Club. Following the arrest of the last group of officers, White called Col. Selway and informed him of what had transpired. Selway ordered him to close the Club again.

This brought the total of officers arrested to 61, a number that Selway never got correct during his calls to First Air Force Headquarters. The arrested officers were restricted to their quarters and the mess halls.

2

Politics and the War Department

The continuing frustration of the black officers in the 477th with its white senior officers was a far cry from the joy that had greeted the birth of the Group a scant two years before. When it was formed, numerous influential blacks across America were gratified. Indeed, many of them had been lobbying long and hard for the formation of just such a unit.

Ironically, our arrest that evening in April 1945 was in a sense an inevitable outcome of a chain of events that actually began the day the senior officers of the 477th Bombardment Group were chosen. An account in some detail of the events as they unfolded, from the beginning, is important in understanding how joyous optimism could deteriorate into frustrated mutiny.

On June 1, 1943, Walter White, Secretary of the National Association for the Advancement of Colored People, received an important telephone call. He must have smiled as he listened to his close friend, and co-fighter in the battle for equal opportunity, A. Philip Randolph. In a voice that would have been filled with joy and pride, Randolph informed White that the Army Air Corps had approved the formation of a black bombardment group.

The NAACP and the black press, led by the nation's most widely read black newspaper, the *Pittsburgh Courier*, were in the forefront of the fight. Other black organizations had also been fighting for full black participation in the armed force's aviation program before and after the approval of a single fighter squadron. The formation of the 99th Pursuit Squadron on March 21, 1941, represented only a small victory in the long battle with the War Department. This limited participation still denied black youth the opportunity to enter the Air Corps and become navigators, bombardiers, aerial gunners, radiomen and flight engineers.

The Negro press of the era, and leaders like Walter White and Robert L. Vann, were not impressed with this superficial effort. Black leaders had decided to settle for no less than full participation in army aviation. On the other hand, the Army Air Corps was resolute against the inclusion of blacks in its ranks.

National politics during this era had powerful influence upon the War Department decisions. The Democratic Party's support by black voters had been on the decline. President Roosevelt was running for an unprecedented third term, and Republican candidate Wendell L. Willkie had declared himself an enemy of racism. Willkie had won the endorsement of Robert Vann's influential *Pittsburgh Courier*. The political ramification of excluding blacks from further participation in the Air Corps had become too severe a negative for politicians, especially the Roosevelt administration. Democrats needed the bloc of black votes, and realized it was advantageous to support blacks' desire for greater Army Air Corps participation.

Birth of the 477th Bombardment Group

As a result of the pressure, the War Department reluctantly agreed to form a medium bombardment group. The unit was designated the 477th Bombardment Group Medium and would be equipped with the B-25J medium bomber aircraft. The addition of this bombardment group substantially expanded the number of air crew positions for blacks.

The air crew training program meant the addition of black multi-engine pilots, as well as navigators, bombardiers, gunners, and radiomen.

Although conservative in nature, the decision to create a Negro combat bomber unit in the Army Air Corps was an upsetting change and at least as stirring a novelty as could be expected in the close-knit and conservative society of the United States Army Air Corps. The decision jarred the Air Corps throughout. A black bombardment group in this rigidly inter-regulated military organization was a major change. This change was felt with diminishing force through every timbre of the United States Army Air Corps.

This decision illustrated three premises. First, it demonstrated the relationship between the public and the government and its delicate sensitivities. Second, it reopened the ancient rivalry between political and military considerations and control. And third, it illustrated exactly what happens when civil and political authorities impose on the army a policy that is only partly in tune with the opinion of the country, but wholly against the grain of the military. This policy divided ideals, loyalties, and purposes.

The selection of the initial commanders of the 477th Bomb Group doomed it from the beginning. There were no black officers with bomber experience, so, of course, the key officers selected as the initial staff for the unit all had to be white. Unlike the 332nd Fighter Group, where promotions to staff and command positions were made as the men gained experience, such advancement would not occur in the 477th. As it turned out, the majority of the white officers was indifferent to the needs of the unit and its black personnel. The 477th came to represent segregation at its worst. Senior white officers devoted the majority of their time and activities more toward the destruction of the 477th rather than to training the unit for overseas deployment. Because of their attitudes and activities, the 477th Bombardment Group never saw combat. It never completed its training for overseas deployment.

The Basic Problem

The 477th Bombardment Group was born on June 1, 1943, but remained a paper outfit until its activation in January 1944. It was a step-child whose foster parents were as reluctant as any parent could be. By no stretch of the imagination were these white supervisors parents. Instead they were a grudging, ersatz substitute.

The father, Gen. Henry H. "Hap" Arnold, Commanding General of the Army Air Forces, tried to abort the unit before it was born, thus implicitly condoning the destructive activities of the ersatz parents throughout the life of the unit.

Col. Robert R. Selway was designated the Commander. A native of Wyoming, and a 1924 graduate of West Point, Selway was considerably older than the World War Two popular image of the dashing young air force officer. Most of the officers of his command were 15 years his junior. A cavalry officer taught to fly by the Army, he still affected the dress of the cavalry officer, including the carrying of a riding crop, or swagger stick. He emitted the aura of an uncompromising authoritarian; he appeared to be permanently at attention. Heavy, bushy eyebrows and flitting eyes gave the impression that he was nervous and unsure of himself. His chronic sniffles and his need to have a Kleenex or handkerchief nearby did not enhance his Air Corps officer appearance.

Selway's hostility toward the whole black bombardment program reflected that of his commander, Maj. Gen. Frank

O' Donnell "Monk" Hunter. Selway was not the officer this new bomber group needed as a commander. He was to find horses a lot simpler than airplanes, and those black trainees who were determined to fly them more difficult.

On the other hand, Selway was a tragic figure in this drama. He wanted to reach the grade of Brigadier General in the worst way, and believed that if he took this bombardment group overseas and into combat, he would reach that goal. He was faced with several choices, all of which interfered with reaching this goal. One was that he wanted to take the group overseas in the format that he designed. He wanted all the top staff positions to be filled by white officers, and blacks to be assigned to the lower-grade positions. It was crucial that the positions which black officers were assigned would not place a black in command of any white personnel. Above all, he had to please his boss, Gen. Hunter.

Hunter commanded the base, the Bomb Group, and First Air Force. He was only slightly younger than Selway. Hunter was a brutal, mean-spirited, undiplomatic general officer who wanted to control every aspect of his command.

A veteran fighter pilot and former leader of American Fighter Forces in Europe, Gen. Ira C. Eaker, now Deputy Commander and Chief of Staff, USAAF, had removed Gen. Hunter as commander of the VIII Fighter Command, in May 1943, for not following Gen. Eaker's directives regarding the use of wing tanks on P-47 fighters.[4] Hunter resented being relieved as a fighter commander. However, in assigning him as Commander of the First Air Force, he was given command of the biggest Air Force in the Army Air Corps. He did not want to be associated with bombers to begin with and, most of all, he resented with all the fiber of his being the association and presence of a group of black fliers that he called a "sideshow".

Hunter, like Selway, still affected the cavalry background, complete with swagger stick. He sported a wild handlebar mustache so heavily waxed it looked artificial. That he was in command of a black bomber group was a very uncomfortable position for him. He was more comfortable treating blacks as he had done in the past, as inferiors, as less than human beings. He was always more comfortable in reacting in the old ways of the white army structure. In short, he preferred using an old map to travel over new terrain.

The Military Lineage of Selway and Hunter

The military had a long history of bias toward the black citizens of this nation. Since colonial times blacks have made increasingly important contributions to America's military might. At first the black soldiers and sailors were few in number, usually serving in time of emergency, and then only as auxiliaries. White colonial militiamen might rely on blacks to clear a parade ground or build a blockhouse, but only when threatened by invasion or Indian attack would they trust the black man with musket, ball, and powder. When given an opportunity to fight, black soldiers and sailors did well, whether in the North American wilderness, at sea, or on foreign battlefields.

Helping defeat America's foes did not gain acceptance for blacks within the military. Traditionally, only a token number of blacks remained in the ranks when the firing died away. Besides fighting the wartime enemy, black Americans faced a second and far more dangerous foe—racism. It is racism that sharply restricted their opportunity within the armed services and in civil society, as well. The accomplishment of blacks in combat, when examined through the distorting prism of white supremacy, all but disappeared.[5]

When World War One began in August 1914, the U. S. Army had no plan to employ the vast reservoir of Negro manpower should the nation become involved in the European conflict. However, following America's entrance into the war in April 1917, the army did undertake to recruit Negro troops totaling more than 400,000. Most Negro soldiers served in the Services of Supply, while others were formed into two infantry divisions and saw action in combat in France. However, their effectiveness was a controversial issue after the war. Ten Army War College classes studied the question of future use of Negro personnel.

The authors of the staff studies believed that blacks had to be employed in a combat role. They stated: "To follow the policy of exempting the Negro population of this country from combat service means that the white population, on which the future of the country depends, would suffer the brunt of the loss, the Negro none..." The Negro, they continued, was "a citizen of the United States, entitled to all of the rights of citizenship and subject to all the obligations of citizenship..." They believed, however, that "no Negro officer should command a white officer." Future studies only muddled the situation, and added additional insults to the Negro citizen.

The Use of Negro Manpower in War, the subject of a War College study concluded on October 30, 1925, included a "Memorandum for the Chief of Staff, U.S. Army." A product of several years study by the faculty and student body of the Army War College, the study was signed by the Commandant of the War College, Maj. Gen. H.E. Ely. It concluded that Negro men believed themselves inferior to white men, that they were by nature subservient, and that they lacked initiative and resourcefulness. If any Negro did score well on intelligence tests, the reason given was that they possessed a "heavy strain of white blood.[6]

"Negro officers," the report claimed, "not only lacked the mental capacity to command, but courage, as well." Their interest was seen as not to fight for their country, but solely to advance their racial interests. Worst of all, according to the report, "the Negro officer was still a Negro, with all the faults and weaknesses of character inherent in the Negro race, exaggerated by the fact that he wore an officer's uniform."[7]

Maj. Gen. Hunter was an unreconstructed advocate of the unwritten policies of the past. He adamantly insisted on having his way in command of black officers. All who knew him, especially the black officers, were aware that he rigidly opposed the mixing of the races. On several occasions he had written and talked about his views. He was aware that blacks hated segregation, yet his prejudice was too fixed to allow that fact to alter his attitude. Worse, he made special efforts to implement and reinforce these attitudes whenever possible.

Retired Lt. Col. Alexander Jefferson, a Tuskegee Airman from Detroit, remembers an incident that occurred during his training at Selfridge while he was flying a gunnery mission:

"The flight pulled up away from the target after a firing pass on the target and rejoined on the leader in perfect V-formation, completing the first pass of the gunnery mission. The flight wheeled around and began to line up for another pass when the radio crackled. 'All officers return to Selfridge and report to the base theater immediately.' I was a brand new second lieutenant, recently graduated from pilot training flying the right wing position. I pressed my mike button and called the flight leader to find out what was going on. 'Hey, Boss, what's up?' 'Hell, Ace, I don't know. I haven't the faintest clue, but we'd better get these birds on the ground.' We headed directly for Selfridge and received landing instructions, as well as instructions to report to the theater as soon as possible. Landing and securing the aircraft, we reported to the base theater and joined our fellow officers, including the white instructors, who were already assembled.

"Almost immediately the group inside the theater was called to attention. The officers snapped to rigid attention. Silence reigned as Hunter strode onto the stage. His wild black handlebar-type mustache bristling, and his riding crop snapped under his arm, he barked, 'At ease!' The officers all sat down. In a voice that eviscerated the hate within, Hunter spoke:

"'The War Department is not ready to recognize blacks on the level of social equal to white men. This is not the time for blacks to fight for equal rights or personal advantages. They should prove themselves in combat first. There will be no race problem here, for I will not tolerate any mixing of the races. Anyone who protests will be classed as an agitator, sought out, and dealt with accordingly. This is my base and, as long as I am in command, there will be no social mixing of the white and colored officers. The single Officers Club on base will be used solely by white officers. You colored officers will have to wait until an Officers Club is built for your use. Are there any questions? If there are, I will deal with them personally.'

"He wheeled about and left the stage."[8]

Col. Selway activated the 477th Bombardment Group at Selfridge Field, Michigan, January 15, 1944. It began without a backlog of trained personnel. Extremely poor planning, disruptive and erratic manning gave the new organization severe disabilities. Yet these impediments paled when compared to the demoralization and disruption caused by the racial antagonism brought on by the command.

Moreover, each new location that was considered for the group was met by local antagonism. Civil leaders and businessmen, in particular, were open in their hostility toward blacks.

Hunter had concluded that the directive issued by Headquarters Army Air Forces Commander Gen. Arnold, that there be a black bomber group trained to go to combat, was a gesture to appease the Roosevelt administration. Hunter felt he did not need to follow the directive. Therefore, he continued with all his considerable skill and cunning to cause the group to fail to reach combat-ready status.

The 477th Stay at Selfridge Field

The 477th Bombardment Group's stay at Selfridge Field, Michigan, was a short but tempestuous one. Col. William Boyd, the Base Commander, was a huge, out-of-shape "country sheriff" type. Resembling a pear more than a trim Air Force officer, his head looked too small for his body. He fought a losing battle to retain white thinning hair on a extremely receding hair line. Horn-rimmed glasses rode far down on his nose, under which nested a trimmed mustache. Instructed to carry out Gen. Hunter's strict orders against any mixing of the races in a social setting, especially in the Officers Club at Selfridge, he went about his charge with unreasonable vengeance. His conduct was the subject of a War Department Inspector's report completed later by Gen. B.O. Davis, Sr. and Col. Harvey Shoemaker. Col. Boyd "forbade Negro officers to use the Officers Club, and employed insulting language in conveying his views on this subject to the Negro officers." Much to Hunter's chagrin, Boyd's action led to an official reprimand for Boyd, who had ordered that the single Officers Club on the base be used solely by whites. The Secretary of War's reprimand to the

Selfridge commander was a particular embarrassment to Hunter, since Boyd had taken this action under orders from Hunter himself. Hunter became very upset that the War Department had issued such a reprimand to Boyd.

Boyd's reprimand was indeed a very sharply-worded document. It stated the following:

"1. Investigation by the Office of the Inspector General has disclosed that racial discrimination against colored officers was due to your conduct in denying to colored officers the right to use the Officers Club. Such action is in violation of Army regulations and explicit War Department instructions on this subject.

"2. As a commissioned officer of the Regular Army of many years standing, you must have had knowledge that your conduct in this respect was highly improper. Not only does your conduct indicate a lack of good judgment, but it also tends to bring criticism upon the military service.

"3. You are hereby formally reprimanded and admonished that any future action on your part will result in your being subjected to the severe penalties prescribed by the Articles of War."[9]

It is important to note that in this reprimand the Secretary of War admitted "that in denying the colored officers the right to use the Officers Club meant that racial discrimination had occurred, and this discrimination was in violation of Army Regulations and explicit War Department instructions on this subject."

Notwithstanding, Hunter wrote an endorsement to the reprimand that strongly rejected its issuance. As a result, he received a call from Lt. Gen. Barney M. Giles, Deputy Commander of the Army Air Forces. In the conversation Giles attempted to convince Hunter to change the endorsement.

"I'd like you to change that, Monk, so we can file it when it gets back here and not have to go to the Secretary of War again," Giles began. "I told General Arnold how you felt about it, and that you didn't want anybody in your command taking the rap for something you condoned."

Hunter attempted to interrupt, shouting, "I didn't condone it. I ordered it."

Giles ignored the interruption and continued, "And that later on, when they were excluded from the club, you went up there and talked to the Commanding Officer and told him to carry it on, and that I concurred in that decision with you. But looking it all over... and I checked in with the War Department here with General McKarney... the endorsement has to be changed, or it will go to the Secretary of War and open the whole thing up again. Then they'll put it on to you. It might even be referred to General Arnold again. I told Arnold that we wouldn't let them join the club, and he approved."[10]

This reprimand should have sent a clear message to Hunter. "Denying to black officers the right to use the Officers Club" was, in the view of the Secretary of War, a violation of Army Regulation 210-10, Paragraph 19. However, again Hunter was deaf to anything that went against his beliefs. The War Department, he thought, would back him if he had separate but equal facilities for blacks and whites. He hastily directed the building of a separate club for the black officers. The building was under construction and completed up to the roof when the War Department ordered all work on the building to stop. Here again, the War Department had sent Hunter a message, and again, Hunter ignored it. He had persisted in pressing the issue of separate Officers Clubs.

Although Hunter was very concerned with the Officers Club problem, he showed little interest in the progress of the

477th. Four months after its formation, the 477th was still at Selfridge Field. Some flying and ground training was going on, but out of an authorized strength of 290 officer crew members, only 175 officers had been assigned. There were almost no navigators and bombardiers included, yet this group was expected to be combat ready within three months. Three months of pre-combat training was the normal time for training a medium bomber group during that wartime period in the Air Force.

The 477th Relocates

On May 5, 1944, without advance notice, all black officers were restricted to the base. All gates to Selfridge were locked. Telephones, radios, and all other means of communication were blocked. The men of the 477th were ordered to board a troop train and move out. They left without knowing where they were going. The train moved in random directions during most of the first night. It went north to Point Huron, crossed to Ontario and traveled across Canada, finally turning back into the United States. The train entered the United States at Buffalo, New York, and headed south toward its final destination, Godman Field, Kentucky. By any standards this was a remarkable route to use to get from Michigan to Kentucky.[11]

Godman Air Field was a small, dilapidated airfield adjoining Fort Knox, Kentucky. Fort Knox was the largest tank training facility in the world. The airfield, associated with Fort Knox, was located across the street from the Fort, and was designed for small liaison type aircraft, not for a medium bomber group. This facility was totally inadequate for the training of the 477th. The bearing capacity of the Godman Field runway surface was only 6,000 to 9,000 pounds, about one-fourth of the bearing capacity required.

Apron space contained a bare 84,000 square yards, about one-fourth the amount of apron space required for the 65 aircraft of the group. One small hangar of 30,000 square feet existed. The longest runway was 5,200 feet, the shortest was 4,500 feet.[12]

The official history of the 477th states that the move was made to take advantage of "better atmospheric conditions for flying." It added that "the housing and maintenance facilities at Godman were adequate." Selfridge had four times the hangar space of Godman Field, seven times the acreage, more extensive runways, five times the gasoline capacity, and better flying weather. Godman could not house the entire group's aircraft because of insufficient hangar or apron space. Its runways had deteriorated, and could not handle the B-25J, the heaviest model of this type of aircraft. Godman Field also lacked an air-to-ground gunnery range.

The War Department never gave a suitable reason for moving the group, or why it chose Godman Field. Should anyone question this move, they would find that Godman had one Officers Club, and Fort Knox was adjacent. The white officers could have quarters at Knox, and be invited to be members of the Knox Officers Club that had no black members, a very cozy arrangement for the white officers assigned to the 477th Bomb Group.

Because of the proximity of Selfridge Field to Detroit, Gen. Hunter and others had felt that most of the racial trouble had been caused by "outside agitators and communistic elements." Godman Field, on the other hand, was somewhat isolated, and in a rural area. Hunter felt certain that at Godman there would be no problem from outside "agitators."

This move conflicted with the War Department's adjustment to the principles of command, and particularly the

command of "Negro troops." The department had published a series of policies and orders which were designed to
tighten the qualifications of white officers assigned to command Negro troops, and they challenged the resistance to
employ Negro officers. These orders laid down the policy
that Negroes should, military necessity permitting, be based
in the north, near communities offering them facilities.
Notwithstanding these directives, the move to Godman was
made.

During the ten months the group was at Godman
Field—May 1944 to March 1945—there was relative peace
at the Officers Club. There was only one Officers Club at
Godman, and anyone could be a member. Any one officer
who did not want to use the club at Godman could use the
Officers Club at Fort Knox. He could that is, if the club at
Fort Knox elected to extend membership to him. Of course,
Fort Knox did not extend membership to any of the black
officers at Godman. They extended "guest memberships"
only to the white officers.

All department heads in the 477th at Godman, including the squadron leaders of the four bombardment squadrons, were white. The operations officers were all white.
While some blacks were named as assistants to the operations officer, no black officer held any position of real
authority. All the command structures of the 477th Bombardment Group were outsiders, from the point of view of
the black community.

A number of black officers had been promised that they
would be advanced to command and supervisory positions
if they would elect to join the bomber unit rather than
continue overseas with the 332nd Fighter Group. This
group consisted of many of the more experienced and
mature, as well as the taller, officers in the Group—the
desired height of fighter pilots was less than six feet. In-

cluded were Bill Ellis, Dick Stanton, C.I. Williams, James T. Wiley, Fitzroy "Buck" Newsum, Daniel "Chappie" James, Peter Verwayne, and Jim Mason, among others. These officers represented the wide range of thinking among the black officers. Representing the "red-hot," eager-to-achieve element were Jim Mason, Bill Ellis, and Daniel "Chappie" James. Others who just wanted to make the group a good fighting group, and who believed that the Army would permit and encourage them to do so, were C. I. Williams, Dick Stanton, James T. Wiley, and "Buck" Newsum. The two groups did not always see eye-to-eye on the importance of morale in the 477th, nor did they completely trust one another. None knew whether the Army Air Force would permit them to prove themselves. Nevertheless, these officers elected transfer to a bomber group from a fighter group.

Those who transferred were sent to Mather Army Air Field in California and Douglas Army Air Field in Arizona for initial B-25 transition training. None of these officers was ever advanced to command positions under the regime of Col. Selway and Gen. Hunter, as promised. The fact gave clear evidence of blatant dishonesty and continuing deceit on the part of the Army Air Force Command structure.

By the first of 1945, the 477th Group's manning was complete. The group was at strength, and could begin combat training. The new combat commitment date for the Group had been adjusted to July 1, 1945.

Back to Freeman Field

Freeman Air Field was a fine air base well suited for the training of the 477th. Since early in January 1945, Gen. Hunter and Col. Selway had been planning to move the group to this base. They had known all along that Godman was inadequate. With the new overseas date they knew that a better, more suitable facility was absolutely essential, particularly if it should turn out that their superiors were serious about meeting this new combat readiness date.

On March 1, 1945, the First Air Force took over Freeman Field, and immediately began to move the major part of the 477th from Godman to Freeman during the first week of March. The group quickly settled into this excellent facility. There was increased eagerness on the part of the bomber crews. The main objective of the fliers was to do some heavy flying to catch up with and meet the new overseas deployment date.

While the airfield was a great asset, the town of Seymour, Indiana, was a serious drawback. Seymour's population of 8,000 people included no more than 75 black civilians. Most were farm hands, porters, and janitors scattered throughout the surrounding area. The community as a whole would not accept or intermingle with the black troops either socially or in their daily business. Restaurants, bars, hotels, and taverns refused to serve them. Typically some local grocery stores refused to sell groceries to wives of the black officers. A few officers and enlisted men attempted to force restaurants to serve them, claiming equal rights since they were members of the United States Armed Services. However, the restaurant owners and merchants remained firm in their refusal. Several of the local merchants in Seymour posted such signs in their windows as "colored will not be served."[13] Rumors had it the town was the founding home of the Ku Klux Klan.

Hunter and Selway remained more concerned with keeping blacks and whites separated than with getting the group ready for combat. They were busily looking for a solution that would meet Hunter's ideas for the complete separation of the races. Freeman Field had a large, luxurious Officers Club—luxurious, that is, by World War II standards, though barely acceptable by present-day standards, but with no Fort Knox club to which they could escape.

Because of Hunter's insistence that there be two Officers Clubs at Freeman Field, Selway wrote a letter order assigning one club for the Overseas Training Unit (OTU) Group, who were all black, and assigning the main Officers Club to permanent party personnel, who were all white. He had taken the main white Non-Commissioned Officers Club and designated it Officers Club Number One for use by OTU group personnel; that is, black officers. The single original Officers Club was designated as Officers Club Number Two, and was reserved for the exclusive use of the white officers. Selway had prepared and issued orders blatantly segregating the clubs by race.

Black officers were not fooled by this stratagem and did not like it one bit! They named the club "Uncle Tom's Cabin," and refused to use it. However, since this club was indeed for OTU, the black officers decided to hold elections for officers for the club. They showed deference to rank and elected Capt. Elmore Kennedy, a senior captain black officer, to be president, though, "hearsay has it," he was not universally liked.[14] They deliberately elected a white squadron commander, Capt. Tyson, of the 619th Bomb Squadron, to the board of directors. This move was a master stroke, and its meaning was not lost on Selway.

The 477th Begins to Resist

On March 10, 1945, two groups of black officers entered the white Officers Club, and ordered drinks and cigarettes. They were refused service and they departed. Some of the officers who visited the club were Lts. Fredericks P. Hicks, Charles H. Drummond, Raymond K. Dewberry, Leslie A. Williams, Ruell Bell, Harold Brown, Dudley M. Glasse, Le

Roy F. Gillead, Leonard E.Williams, George Peters, Ted Moran, and Celestino S. Monclave, and F/Os Charles Wilson and Frank V. Pivalo.[15]

The visit of these officers to the club caused Selway great concern. Both he and Hunter had not been very confident that the plan for separating the black and white officers would work. Selway was very nervous about his position as the enforcer of this plan, as well as concerned about the strength of the backing of Hunter. Hunter was an explosive man, and very difficult to talk with.

At 10:00 a.m., on March 10, 1945, Hunter called Selway. This call did nothing to boost Selway's confidence. At the beginning of their conversation, Selway thought that Hunter was actually concerned with his health when Hunter asked, "How's everything?" Selway began to give him a status of his health, only to have Hunter interrupt to inquire about the situation there in reference to the club and the black officers.

The transcripts of this telephone conversation make crystal clear that Hunter had very little confidence in Selway. He did not think Selway knew how to handle this kind of a situation. Selway sensed Hunter's lack of confidence and tried to think ahead. He offered information he thought would increase Hunter's confidence in him. In his effort Selway even went so far as to indicate that he had black officer spies within the 477th. He thought that because of these spies he would know in advance what would be happening in the future. Consequently, Hunter should have had more faith in his opinions and actions.[16]

Following the incident at Club Number Two on March 10, 1945, the black officers took no further actions involving this club, yet the threat of further incursions remained. Since nothing was planned, Selway was not getting any real news, and was losing confidence in his spies. This only increased his apprehension.

Selway was very unsure of the legality of his order. He kept whining to Hunter that he was unsure that his order was legal. Both Hunter and Selway knew in their hearts that the order was not legal, but Hunter assured Selway that if he neither mentioned color nor race, they would be on firm ground. Hunter himself was not so sure, and he decided to send his legal representatives out to Freeman to check the order for legality. Should the order not check out, the legal staff would write a new one. Selway had in mind an order that would do more than keep the white and black officers apart in clubs. He wanted an order that would prevent any mixing of the two groups in any type of social circumstance. The order, furthermore, would have to be formulated in such form that it would not bring down the wrath of the War Department.

The conspirators knew they needed to write a brand new order, yet writing this would prove harder than they had anticipated. They wanted it to have real strength and finesse to do the job, and, at the same time, be legal. On the other hand, how could any order be designed to accomplish this task and be legal when any such order would immediately violate Army Regulation 210-10, Paragraph 19?

The All-Important Army Regulation 210-10, Paragraph 19

All Army officers clubs were supposed to operate without restrictions. There existed a regulation—Army Regulation 210-10, dating from 1940—that specifically opened the officers clubs on all posts, bases, and stations to all officers.

When this regulation was written, there were only five black officers in the regular Army. The two Davises (Col. Benjamin O. Davis, Sr. and 1st Lt. Benjamin O. Davis, Jr.) and three chaplains. This regulation was written more to prevent officers clubs from barring certain units rather than individuals. This regulation did not consider race, inasmuch as it did not foresee an increase in black officers in the service. The Army felt that local exclusionary policies would take care of the problem.[17]

As the Air Corps begin training pilots and officers at Tuskegee, and at Officers Candidate Schools, there was an increase in the black officer population in the Army Air Forces and other Army services. Most armed forces officers clubs routinely excluded black officers ignoring Paragraph 19 of AR 210-10. They simply refused to be bound by the rules included in this regulation, which clearly approved the admission of all officers, including black officers.

Thus AR 210-10 is one of the most important documents that relates to the Freeman Field Mutiny. Likewise, the most important paragraph of that regulation is Paragraph 19. As this regulation became the foundation of black officers' protests to their exclusion from officers clubs, the Army thought there was a need for further directions that could rectify the problem. As a result, the Adjutant General of the Army, Maj. Gen. J. A. Ulio, made his contribution by writing a very soft term letter designed to remedy the problem. In this letter, he gave even more explicit instructions against segregation. He directed that all personnel, regardless of race, would be afforded the opportunity to enjoy recreational facilities on each post, camp, and station.

The First Attempt at an Order

The First Air Force Air Staff worked hard on Selway's new order. Col. Torgils G. Wold, Air Inspector of the First Air Force, made several recommendations designed to control the officers, including the readiness of the white MP unit, and a new and more vigorous command. In desperation, he even considered the possibility of "Negro command." Yet, he felt that should the command accede to a portion of the black officers' campaign at this time, he warned, "this might lead to further unacceptable demands."[18]

This new order started with the old, wide-meshed arrangement of assigning separate facilities to separate units. For example, as previously mentioned, one club was assigned for permanent party, and one for the 477th and the Combat Crew Training Squadron that would be arriving later from Godman. In addition, the order introduced a refinement. It separated facilities by supervisor versus trainee. These two principles were laminated into a single phrase: OTU (Overseas Training Unit) and CC (combat crew) Trainee Officers Recreational Building.

This arrangement would save the white squadron commander, who had been elected to the board of Club Number One, from tearing his hair out. He was a member of the OTU. That put him in the black club, but his not being a trainee got him out again. It was understood that white OTU officers would be regarded as supervisors, not trainees. They were all key officers. As a refinement on Selway's original OTU officers' definition, this was not bad, but it was not perfect. Unfortunately for Selway, some of the key officers on the record were black. The personnel strength at Freeman Field included some 700 officers: 292 white and 422 black. In the enlisted ranks were 3,424: 721 white and 2,703 black.

The new order contained several confused and unde-fined specifications. It combined the force of a definitive order with the intangibility of informal discretion. For instance: "Personnel, commissioned and enlisted, will use the... recreational facilities... as designated in paragraph two; and at the times and within the restrictions as may be required by the custodians of the buildings and areas, upon approval by the base commander." Would custodians know supervisors when they saw them?

This provision served another purpose. It could carry any negative implications that might be necessary for the order to bear. For it was one thing to assign a club to a unit; it was another, and more ticklish maneuver, to prohibit another unit from coming into that club. It would be hard to make the prohibition tight enough without running up against the War Department policy. Thus the legal achieve-ment of the order is simply eclectic. Its literary achievement was just as eclectic, but finer.[19]

"This assignment of buildings is based on the AAF (Army Air Forces) Standards governing the control of per-sonnel in the training of units, the development of the individual and the unit combat spirit of personnel undergo-ing OTU and combat crew training, and necessary for the conservation of fuel and power," the order began. It cleverly omitted citing any AAF Regulations or Standards. It plunged immediately into peripheral stringency, setting a military tone: "Only those buildings will be used which can be utilized, to the maximum extent, by compact organization of units and personnel, and buildings not required will remain closed and locked." After the sentence ordering the use of the facilities as designated, there came more realistic detail about engineers and surveys.

One of the more obvious defects to this order was the address. It was addressed to "All Organization Commanders, All Officers in Charge of Sections and Activities." That was not good enough. The fliers from Godman, having not been addressed, could not be presumed to have read it.

On April 1, 1945, Selway published, but did not sign, this new letter order. In fact, he would later disown it. For a while it seemed that this new order was working. Selway at least thought so. The black officers stayed away from the white club, and flew "the pants off those airplanes that they had," he joyfully told Hunter.

3

Hot Telephones

On April 6, 1945, the day after the first 36 of us had been arrested, the telephone lines between Freeman Field and Headquarters First Air Force suddenly got hot. This increased telephone traffic continued to accelerate throughout the crisis. At the same time, traffic also increased to Headquarters Army Air Forces at the Pentagon.

The immediate reaction to the mutiny by Gen. Hunter and Col. Selway was to figure out what had hit them. Their next problem was to determine how to regain control of the situation, all the while continuing to segregate, as well as discriminate against, the black members of the 477th Bombardment Group.

It was apparent that Selway was not aware of all that had happened. He was not given details about the incursion at the Club while it was happening that night. It was not until the next morning, the 6th of April, that he was informed. Even then he was given only a minimal briefing. Notwithstanding, Selway hurried to contact Hunter in order to demonstrate that he was in control of the situation. However, the news of the activities of the night before had already reached First Air Force Headquarters, and, before he could call Hunter, Gen. Glenn, the Chief of Staff First Air Force, was on the line to Selway demanding to know what the hell was going on out there. Selway, relying on the hasty briefing he had been given, made a dispirited effort to give Glenn a complete story. He was acutely aware that he was expected to be fully informed about what had occurred; yet he had only a vague account of the events that had taken place.

Selway began, "It looks like at about 2030 hours two groups of personnel from the newly-arrived Combat Crew Training Squadron black officers came down to the Officers Club Number Two, that's the white Officers Club. Nineteen of them were in one group and the rest in the other group." *That was his first mistake. There had been three groups of officers that had entered the Club and had been arrested.* "I had ordered all the doors closed except one main entrance. They were met outside by the Club Officer, the Officer of the Day, and by their immediate Squadron Commander, Capt. Chiappe, who was in command of the squadron at the base, that's Replacement Training personnel." *This was the second mistake. Chiappe was nowhere around at the beginning.* "They were informed then that the facilities of that club, according to my orders, were for base supervisory officers, and they were not to enter because they had been assigned by the same order their own club and lounge, and mess facilities; yet they said they were going to enter anyway. The Assistant Provost Marshal gave them a direct order in the name of the Commanding Officer not to violate that order. They pushed him aside and came in anyway. Then Chiappe lined them up. He told them he was in command of their squadron, and that he would take it up with the Commanding Officer in the morning, and to leave immediately. So they did." *That was the third mistake. The first group was lined up by the Club Officer, Maj. White, and arrested when they refused to leave.*

Gen. Glenn wanted to know how many officers had been involved and Selway guessed at the number as being 33. *The actual number had been 36.* Selway continued in his effort to seem informed on the incident. "So I asked General Hunter if I could charge them under two articles, as they claimed ignorance of the regulations assigning the buildings. Before they entered, a senior officer told them about the order, and told them that it included not just OTU personnel of the Bomb Group, but CCTS personnel, also. So, I'll charge them under the 64th, I think... I've forgotten which. I told Hunter."

"Have you provided them with adequate club facilities for their use?" Glenn asked.

"I've set up what I thought was decent facilities, and General Haynes was out there and inspected them with me, and thought they were swell. Theirs is divided into three different buildings whereas the base officers have to have theirs in one building, and General Haynes seemed to be very favorably impressed with facilities assigned them."

Actually there was a marked difference in the two buildings. Officers Club Number Two had a game room with billiard tables, card tables, and table tennis tables. Also, there was a large fireplace in the main lounge. Officers Club Number One had no game room, no table tennis tables, or billiard tables. There was no guest house associated with the facility, as was with Club Number Two. Club Number Two had the mess hall attached, Club Number One did not have a mess hall. Contrary to what Selway tried to imply, the facilities assigned for use by the black officers was markedly inferior to the officers club assigned for use by the white officers.

Selway continued: "So we are drawing up the orders— we have read the building assignment order to them again, got the Squadron Commander to read it to them again, and they were told that it was the command of the Commanding General of the First Air Force. That's what Hunter told me to tell them, and that it had been coordinated with Army Air Forces, and it was policy on numerous other Air Force training stations within the continental United States—that is, that base and supervisory officers have certain facilities, and those undergoing training have different facilities. So, I told him then that I wanted to charge them under the 64th for willful disobedience of an order, and the other charges under the 66th, because we may be able to prove they were organizing such a stand, that's an additional article. They are being ordered into arrest in quarters and we are preferring the charges as rapidly as we can, and, as soon as it is investigated, I'm going to have it flown up to First Air Force."

Glenn replied, "That's good. All right, now, I'll get our Judge Advocate over so I can have him hear the record of this thing. It might be that he can give you some additional advice on the preparation of charges under the Articles you selected. Would that be of help to you?"

Selway, always trying to be the ultimate team player, nevertheless did not want too much help from First Air Force. But he did want to be cooperative. "Well, Captain Reddin, my legal officer, is pretty good, and I think your Judge Advocate should call him. I know just so much law, and if there is some comment there I'd rather he'd call him."

"I think you're right. Is there anything else you want us to do?"

"I don't know," Selway said, "Trying to send in some military police thing or something would rile it up. This is an organization of Negro officers."

"Okay, go ahead," Glenn said.

Selway could not resist a chance to appear more knowledgeable about the whole situation. However, his comments, like those of many of his contemporaries, makes it clear that he was completely ignorant of what this protest was all about.

Selway raced on: "All of this has given plenty of evidence of being backed by the Society for the Advancement of the Race, and we thought it was very peculiar that a reporter from this Negro paper in Indianapolis slipped in here yesterday and did not report in or anything, and went all among them, and when I found out about it I had to practically physically take him off the post. He came in as an agitator, and it seem this was organized in advance that he was supposed to be here and write it all up. We got him off the post, and I told him anything he wanted to write about this organization he should apply to the War Department."

"Did this occur before they attempted to force their way into the Club? Was he put off the post before that?" asked . Glenn.

"Well, he had been here most of the day, and my Intelligence people said he insisted on seeing me. Well, I give no interviews without the authority of the War Department, and they had to take him in a car and take him off the post. But he was on here without authority; he had no permission from higher headquarters."

The reporter that Selway was discussing was Lowell M. Trice, the very active head of the Indianapolis National Association for the Advancement of Colored People, and a reporter for the black *Indianapolis Recorder*. Selway felt that Trice was present at Freeman Field in connection with a deliberately planned incident.

"He wasn't with them, was he?" asked Glenn. "He was not on the post at the time that these 33 men tried to force their way into the Club."

Selway did not know, but he tried to make it seem that he was on top of the situation, "Well, let's see, we got him off the post about six or seven, and I'd gone to bed, and this thing I guess happened about 9:30, and they told me about it this morning."

"Yes?"

"Four of them had come by previously, and the Club Officer told me that they had not tried to enter, they had just been out on the roadway, and he told them it was not assigned for their use, and they went on. This other incident of the officers entering the Club happened later on in the evening. The personnel of the Group seem highly pleased with the station and are getting on with their flying training and maintenance is good and everything, but I do believe that these papers are riling them up, as far as I am concerned, as an individual. All the articles pick on me and General Hunter as the symbols of segregation. As individuals they seem to like the dances and shows and work," suggested Selway.

The black press was right on target, but it was not the papers that "riled us up."

Gen. Glenn continued in his attempt to bolster Selway's sagging morale. "Well, I'm sure you're doing everything you can. I wouldn't get excited about the thing at all. You can rest assured General Hunter will back you to the limit on the action you've taken, and Washington knows about it, too, so just keep us advised and this headquarters will back you to the limit," Glenn added.

"A little help that you could give is a few more white military police—that wouldn't look like we were ordering anything in—for security purposes. You see, I've shipped out so many, I only have about six or eight white MPs, and I had to leave a few down at Godman because I had to maintain that base as a sub-base, and we've taken all the colored out and left the white down there," replied Selway.

"You have only six or eight white MPs?" asked Glenn.

"Well, just on the gate. I'm not going to pull the colored off because there are some good ones there, but they're kind of supervisors, you know, but eight or ten good white MPs could be ordered in as individuals to head up the guard section.

"All right, I'll see what we can do on that," replied Glenn.

"I'll keep you informed of what goes on," Selway added.

"If anything comes up at all, General Hunter wants to have a general officer down there to help you, he may send General Haynes, or, if necessary, he'll come down himself. You just keep us informed all the time. I think that's everything, Selway. Thank you," said Glenn, as he ended the conversation.[20]

The events surrounding the firing and reprimand to Colonel Boyd at Selfridge AFB were still fresh in Selway's mind, and he did not want to lose his head in this fight. He felt the black officers could be manipulated. Supporting this idea was the handling of Lt. John Silvera, and other black officers that Selway felt were agitators. It was amusing that he thought Silvera wanted to give him "proof of loyalty." Selway had reported him to headquarters as one of "the new race agitators," and had singled him out along with a group of five officers to be spied on, investigated, and shadowed, including threats of reclassification or court-martial. He had transferred Silvera from Freeman back to Godman. The group singled out included Capt. Redden, the Executive Officer of the 616th Squadron, Lt. James C. Flowers, and Lt. Lester B. Norris. An interesting fact is all these officers were classified as Intelligence Officers. When this report first surfaced, Maj. E.G. Gammon, O&T Bomb FAF, stated on July 17, 1944, in a material and supply sectional file in a handwritten note, that Selway was court-martialing one and reclassifying the other three, as well as two others. However, there was no report of further action on this matter. Incidentally, Silvera was not arrested at any time during this entire incident.[21]

Selway Tries to Save Face with His Superiors

Col. Selway knew that he had failed to give a good report to Gen. Glenn in his earlier conversation. After another group of officers had entered the club and been arrested, and after he had received further briefing on the incident, Selway decided to call and try again. He began by saying, "We have had some more trouble here, after the squadron commander read the orders to them, today 21 of them *(actually 25)* paraded down and went into the club. So we are rounding up those veins *(a word often used when referring to blacks)*, and I will write arrest orders on those and, of course, start charges. Now we are going to be a little jammed in this legal department out here."

"Fifty-seven of them?" asked Glenn.

"There were 36 and 21 more this afternoon."

"That makes a total of 57," pondered Glenn. *(The total was 61.)*

"I haven't added it. I just got back from the hangars and they told me about it. I am gathering up the names now as I am concerned about this. One of the 36 put in arrest, we can't find him. I don't know what the attitude of the rest of them will be, but have had the detention board in the hospital, and they are putting up 36 bunks. So, I can take care of those. Now comes the 21, and there is no room there and the guardhouse is full. *(No officers were in the guardhouse.)* We are going to need some legal help out here to help type them all up. I'm going to close up this club, and just open the back for mess. I thought maybe we could get some legal help from the First Air Force."

Glenn was willing to help. "All right, give me some idea of what you want."

Selway suggested that Glenn send the Assistant Judge Advocate, Maj. Osborn, "and if you have any legal clerks— we have two, but now that they have added charges on each one of them, any spare clerks that you have will help."

Glenn said that he "would talk to our Judge Advocate and see how he is fixed, and see what we can send… I imagine two or three clerks anyway."

Selway was in a quandary because the regulation required that when charging persons with court-martial offenses, the charging officer was supposed to serve them as quickly as possible. A possible solution was to get clerical help from some nearby stations sent over to Freeman. Selway cautiously asked Glenn, "What would you advise in case all of them are placed in arrest? Should this happen I just can't take care of them properly."

"No, you can't," agreed Glenn.

On second thought Selway added, "Some of the officers in the group don't seem to be involved in this thing—it just seems as though there is a clan. These four officers that just came by the Club on the afternoon of the fifth of April, came by quietly and did not attempt to enter the Club. They look as if they were simply trying to make a test of their social equality.

"Yes, the whole works will probably try it."

"I don't think there is any violence contemplated."

"As long as they are inviting it, each one that tries it, you will have to add him to the list. I don't know where you are going to put them all, though."

"The white people here are watching while we make the arrests."

Selway, still concerned about his military police strength, asked, "Has there been any action taken to strengthen my MP forces?"

Glenn replied, "I have already told Personnel about getting you some more MPs down there, white ones."

"Good, we may need them at any moment."

Glenn, attempting to sum up the situation, said, "I hardly think so. I think you are probably correct. It is just going to be a test case is all, and the few agitators have probably talked many of the other officers into it. I don't think you will have any difficulty or violence with them at all. In fact, once the Bomb Group had the order read to them, they stayed out."

"I do think it might be advisable for General Haynes to get down there pretty quick, don't you?"

"I think so; yet I think I'm doing everything right."

"Yes, I know that, but sometimes it would help a little bit to have a general officer get the whole bunch together and talk to them," Selway suggested.

"Prestige. If they wanted a test case of it, enough of them have done it, and now I think they will now mind their own business."

"I'll talk to General Hunter. He is here now about that, and probably will have General Haynes down there very shortly."

"All the rest of them seem to be going about their jobs, saluting and everything. It was, therefore, definitely cooked up off this station. They cooked it up before they came here. They planned the whole thing down at Godman. They just had the thing arranged I think, and they wanted it to come off when that reporter was here, but I got wise and got him off the post, but it will break out all over the papers anyway."

"I will get busy on this and see what we can get in the way of help down to you right away, clerical help, and to get them sent down with General Haynes if he comes down."

"Now if they break, all of them break their arrest, I wonder..." Glenn said.

"Just simply additional charges, that is all."

"Additional charges, but I mean a question of securing the bodies."

"If they all take off, they are still AWOL until you catch them."

"O.K., I'll keep you informed."

"Fine. Thanks a lot."[22]

4

Selway Wants More Charges

Col. Selway was committed to satisfying Gen. Hunter by court-martialing the black officers. However, he was uncertain as to which article of the Manual for Courts-Martial he would use. From rumors he believed that the incursion into the club had been planned at Godman Field, and he concluded that there was a conspiracy. Therefore, he wanted to use two articles, one to cover the disobedience of an order, and another to cover the conspiracy.

While he was contemplating his course of action, Col. Torgils G. Wold and Maj. Harry V. Osborne, Jr., from the Judge Advocate's Office, First Air Force, arrived at Freeman on April 6, 1945, to conduct an investigation. As a result of Col. Wold's investigation, and on the advice of Maj. Osborne, the matter no longer seemed so clear cut. The two believed that, technically, there was a case against each of these officers, but that there was a remote chance of a misunderstanding. They concluded that only the three officers who had been accused of jostling the Assistant Provost Marshal should be tried. They further recommended that all of the officers arrested on April 5 and 6, with the exception of the three accused of jostling, be released from arrest in quarters.

With an eye to the future, they suggested that a more detailed order in the form of a base regulation be written and published. The new regulation would cover the assignment and uses of these facilities with a view of eliminating the possibility of any misunderstanding of the order. However, implementing this decision was a complex undertaking and required numerous additional telephone calls between the different headquarters.

A casual reading of the report of the arrest suggests that we were being held in the "guardhouse." We were not. We were in arrest in our Bachelor Officers Quarters. However, Hunter and Selway were thinking about using more restrictive facilities if more officers were arrested.

Selway felt that he could go a long way in pleasing Hunter by using as many charges as he could. This way, more black officers would be liable for court-martial. Our planning had considered this possible move. We knew one element that was definitely in our favor—numbers. The more of us who were arrested, the greater the publicity, and the increased likelihood of public pressure. Selway had originally charged the 61 black officers arrested with violation of the 69th Article of War. In a later telephone conversation with Hunter, Selway mused, "Since I got this evidence this morning that they had organized this thing in advance at Godman, I think I can charge them under the 66th, which is mutiny, and sedition should be added."

Since Hunter was interested in additional charges, he replied, "All right. You can prepare anything you want. My Judge Advocate General will study it."

Selway explained to Hunter, "Colonel Wold and Major Osborn are out here, and advise me that I've got technical cases against these people, but not iron-bound cases, and they think that there are only three of them that I can convict. Those are the ones that pushed the Assistant Provost Marshal. So it looks like I'm going to have to release the rest. Now, I was wondering whether we could get you to appoint a special general court. In other words, instead of using the standard general court out here, we could appoint another one."

This idea did not catch the fancy of Hunter. He replied, "Well, what's the matter with the standard one?"

"For example, like you did on that case at Selfridge Field, and have one of your good legal members…" What Selway was looking for was a repeat of some shenanigans that had been used before in a court case at Selfridge Field.

Hunter had to refresh his memory, but when he did, he liked the idea better and added, "Oh, yes, we can do all that. You send the thing on in here and we'll give it full consideration."

Selway was delighted, and he added, "And the TJA and everybody else." The TJA (Trial Judge Advocate) is the law officer on a military court. He rules on the law and plays a very important part in the outcome of a court-martial case. What Selway was looking for was a special "packed" court to try any cases resulting from the arrest being made. Hunter agreed.

Selway was satisfied that he had won this point. Having consolidated his position, he began to wax philosophically, "It looks like they're trying to test this thing." But his comfortable position was short-lived.

Hunter began to chastise him: "Now I can't understand why you didn't get out an order when I sent you that. Also, you didn't have a copy of that teleprinter message I sent you approving of your Officers Club assignments. You didn't bring that down from Godman, did you?"

"We had the telegram up here, but it had been sent to Godman, you know, and decoded there, and I knew what was in it and it confirmed our telephone conversation."

Hunter grew angry. He could not forgive Selway for this dereliction. "That's right. Now I'm sorry that you hadn't published an order other than this assignment of buildings, because those people don't see that. "

"They all knew about it, and the Officer of the Day in front of the Club told them that they were included—they'll deny the fact that they heard the OD. They've got a man who's a lawyer behind them, General, and anything we write, they're going to go out and test that."

"All right, but I want it written so that they are disobeying orders if they don't do it..."

"Did General Haynes show you that draft that Colonel Wold drew up?" Selway asked.

"I've got it here, and there are some things I don't like about it."

"And it ought to be written to actually forbid them to enter the building, because they'll claim that they're not using the facilities, that they're going in there looking for their instructor."

"They can be instructed that they will not use the building, that the assignment of these recreational facilities are as follows: Base Supervisory personnel, and that it does include certain officers in the group and squadrons who are instructor-officers, will use one club, and the others considered as trainees will use the other club. I got a decision before when I sent you that TWX (telegraphic message). I got a decision from Washington, the Air Inspector, and from the Air Judge Advocate General. They said that it was perfectly proper. Now I've talked to General Schneider, and told him to look it up and get me something in writing on it, but you are fully covered, I think, in that message I sent you, but I'll send you another one."

"Well, I refer to it right up here at the top, based on AAF standards." Selway said, attempting a reply.

"I'll send you a definite TWX that you can refer to in this thing."

"If we rewrite it, General, more specifically and state the certain buildings that they will not enter, because they're going to enter them and claim they're not using the facilities."

"Yes, you can get out a post order that certain buildings will be used by trainees, and certain buildings by the permanent party, and that they will refrain from entering those buildings, and the order will be for both of them. Don't mention colored or white."

"How about the wording, General, that they will refrain from entering those buildings except on official business?"

"That's right."

"Then, obviously, if they come down in a mass, they couldn't be coming in there on official business."

"I would like a copy of any order you get out sent up here, and I'll send it down to Washington to get it okayed. I don't like your closing up the club."

"Well, I ran out of space, you know. I wouldn't have had any place to put them," pleaded Selway.

"You've got some quarters."

"I had them in arrest in quarters, all of them, but if they had all broken it, I didn't…"

"Well, if they had broken it, you can still put them there and keep them under guard, and if that don't work, we can send them back to Godman," Hunter replied.

(This is where the idea of returning to Godman first came up, a decision that will later become most significant.)

"Are they going to take that draft and send me down something, or do you want me to draw up something and send it up there?" Selway asked.

"I have this thing here. I wasn't going to actually get it down to you until I had heard from Washington."

"What I'll do then is go ahead and charge these three, release the rest and put them back in training, and then sit tight until I get something from you."

"Yes. You can tell them right now that the Commanding General of the First Air Force says that the trainees will use one club, and the permanent party, which includes the instructor personnel in that group, will use another club."

"And that they will not enter the other except on official business."

"That's right, and that goes for both. For the permanent party, and also for the others."

"Then I can go ahead and open the Club then? "

"Certainly."

"Well, I wanted to get something that was ironbound, that you approved, before I stuck our necks out again."

"I don't like closing the Club, that's a weakness right there. I'd open the Club, but I'd get this order out, and when you write the order you can call me up and read it to me on the phone."

"O.K., Sir."[23]

The legal staff would now rewrite the old order. The new, stronger, ironbound, cleverly-worded base regulation was sure to force compliance by the black officers. The staff was successful in creating the new regulation, but subsequent events made clear that it did not live up to all expectations.

Base Regulation 85-2

Selway followed Hunter's order and released the original group of arrested officers, with the exception of the three officers who were being held for jostling the Provost Marshal.

The same day, April 9, 1945, Selway called Hunter to read him the suggested Base Regulation, written with the help of Col. Wold and Maj. Osborne. As one might conjecture, this regulation had been very hard to write. Hunter wanted the new regulation to have strength, but finesse—strength that would suppress and diffuse the new aggressiveness being demonstrated by the black officers, and finesse that would ensure its legality. Its intent, of course, was no different from the original regulation. It sought to bar black officers from using Officers Club Number Two.

The two officers discussed the minute details of the wording, such as the use of the phase, "Army Air Forces standards," versus "Army Air Forces policy." Then Hunter suggested that each officer be given a copy, and that each officer sign for it. They agreed further that each officer would be required to sign a statement that he had read and understood the regulation.[24]

This was their fatal mistake. This requirement provided the black officers with a formidable weapon to use in resisting this order.

"Now Will You Sign?"

Early in the afternoon on April 10, 1945, the call went out for all officers to report to the base theater at 1500 hours. In groups of ten or twenty or more the black officers moved toward the base theater. At the appointed hour all officers had assembled. We looked at each other with quizzical expressions that said, "What now?" We were soon to find out.

Down front and to the left of the stage at a long table sat three white officers, all of them looking very stern. Lt. Col. John B. Pattison, the Deputy Commander of the 477th Bombardment Group, began to read the new Base Regulation 85-2. He explained in great detail each and every paragraph. He carefully explained that this regulation was necessary to conduct the combat training for our bomb group. After reading the regulation, Lt. Col. Pattison gave each officer a copy, and directed that they read and sign the endorsement thereon.

All the officers accepted the regulation, and some read it, but no one signed the endorsement. A standoff ensued. The endorsement was like a certificate, and should each officer sign it, he would be signifying that he had read and fully understood the regulation. In addition, signing this endorsement would indicate that each officer intended to obey it.

After a few moments of silence, while we were supposedly reading the regulation, Lt. Col. Pattison asked, "Does any one have any questions?" The group of white officers waited eagerly for someone to speak. No one said a word. The silence was deafening. This was our planned response. During any group meetings no one was to speak out, ask questions, or answer questions. This was a forced defensive move. Pattison's question was a familiar strategy. It was customary for the senior officer in a confrontational situation to attack anyone who would speak, and in some way force that person into a position where he could be charged with insubordination. When the silence continued, the group of white officers grew more and more uncomfortable and unhappy. They were mystified at our behavior and resistance. The meeting was abruptly dismissed.

The following day Capt. Chiappe, the Commander of Squadron E selected the names of 14 officers who would not certify that they had read the regulation. He called the officers in for a group interview. He advised them that they could delete any words they choose from the prepared endorsement, or that they could prepare their own endorsement stating simply that they had read it. Only three of these officers did so. The remaining eleven refused to sign any statement that they had read the regulation. Chiappe terminated this interview session and awaited the big push by Selway to get the black officers to sign the regulation. I was not included in this initial group interviewed by Chiappe.

Selway conferred with the Air Inspector, First Air Force, and the Judge Advocate Assistant, Maj. Osborne, over the failures. They advised him that the best way to determine whether these officers understood this action and the meaning of it in the military sense was to set up a special board. This board would consist of two black officers, and two white officers, the base legal officer, a secretary to record the proceedings, and the commanding officer of the officer being interviewed. All officers would appear before this board as individuals for a personal interview. Members of this board would serve as witnesses during the interview. In each case, the officer being interviewed would be given a direct order by his commanding officer to sign Base Regulation 85-2. The legal officers were satisfied that if the officer was given the opportunity to strike out the phrase "and fully understand," and design his own statement indicating that he had read the order, the officer would sign.

Should the officer still refuse to sign, after being given an order to sign the regulation by his commander, the officer would then be in violation of the 64th Article of War. This article covers the offense of disobeying a direct order of a superior officer in time of war, and upon conviction carries a penalty of death. As the staff legal officer read the plan, one can just imagine Selway listening with glee, greatly enjoying what he was hearing. This procedure must surely be the tool that was needed to take the measure of these "trainees."[25]

5

The Arrest of the 101

Col. Selway followed these suggestions to the letter. He formed his board as suggested by Maj. Osborn. The two black officers he selected were Lt. Frank "Slick Nick" Roberts and Capt. James Pughsley. I had known Lt. Roberts since my high school days in Evanston, where he was a student at Northwestern University. In a chance meeting the afternoon of April 9, we discussed his position. In defense of himself he stated that he "had no alternative but to follow orders." I explained that I saw him "as part of the enemy now and no longer as a friend."

Others members of this committee included three white officers—Lt. Col. John B. Pattison, Lt. Col. Thomas C. Keach, and the base Judge Advocate General—each black officer's commander, and the base legal officer, Capt. Ochs, or, in his absence, his assistant, 1st Lt. Dwight R. Kinder. When an officer appeared before this board, the interview was conducted by either Ochs or Kinder.

On April 11, 1945, all black officers were told to stand by for a call to meet with their commanding officer at the base legal office. During the day, each officer was individually directed to report to the legal office. There did not seem to have been any order in which we were being called to appear before the board. A large number of officers and flight officers were subsequently interviewed. Many refused to sign Base Regulation 85-2. My turn came at 1500 hours.

It would be impossible to know how each of the officers responded while appearing before the board. One thing is certain, though. One hundred officers refused to sign the regulation or a separate endorsement. There can be no doubt about this fact—because, after the interviews, 101 of us were arrested.

The following is a true copy of the transcript of my interview including the direct questions that I was asked during my appearance before the board and my full answers:

Transcript of F/O Warren, James C., T-131958, 1500 hours.

Lt. Kinder: Have you read Base Regulation 85-2?

F/O Warren: I have no statement, Sir.

Kinder: I'll hand you Base Regulation 85-2 and you may read it.

(F/O Warren read the regulation.)

Lt. Kinder: Now, have you read Base Regulation 85-2?

Warren: Sir, I do not wish to make a statement.

Kinder: Are you familiar with the provisions of the 64th Article of War?

Warren: I have no statement, Sir.

(Lt. Kinder read aloud the 64th Article of War)

Kinder: Is there any question in your mind about the 64th Article of War?

Warren: No, Sir.

Kinder: Do you fully understand it?

Warren: I have no statement to make, Sir.

Capt. Chiappe: F/O Warren, I, as your Commanding Officer, order you to read aloud Base Regulation 85-2.

(F/O Warren read aloud Base Regulation 85-2.)

Kinder: Now, F/O Warren, do you desire to make a certificate to the effect that you have read Base Regulation 85-2?

Warren: No, Sir.

Kinder: Do you care to write up your own certificate stating whatever you wish to say?

Warren: I have no statement to make, Sir.

Chiappe: I, as your Commanding Officer, order you to certify in writing that you have read Base Regulation 85-2. Do you intend to carry out the order I have given you? Answer "Yes, Sir" or "No, Sir."

Warren: Do I have to answer under the 24th Article of War? I have no statement to make, Sir.

Chaippe: You are placed in arrest of quarters and will remain so until I tell you otherwise. You will use your own barracks, latrine, and mess hall. Is that clear?

I made no answer, saluted and left the room.[26]

Until I was able to read these now declassified records, I had always wondered what happened during the questioning of the other officers. The following questions came to my mind: Did they sign the Base Regulation, or did they sign some other form of certificate that satisfied the power structure? Had all officers been given the opportunity to sign or refuse to sign the Base Regulation before this committee?

Six officers chose to explain their reason for refusing to sign the regulation. Two, 2nd Lts. Le Roy R. Gillead and Herbert J. Schwin, were interviewed in the presence of Capt. Ochs on April 11. Neither would state whether he had read the regulation. After the 64th Article of War had been read and explained to them, both refused to comply with the direct order given them by Capt. Chiappe to read the regulation. These two officers were charged with willful disobedience of the lawful command of Chiappe to read Base Regulation 85-2.

One officer, 2nd Lt. Samuel Colbert, replied, "No comments," when asked by Ochs to state whether or not he had read the regulation. Chiappe then handed him a copy of the regulation and ordered him to read it, but he again said, "No comments," when asked whether he had read it. He remained silent when given a direct order by Chiappe to read the regulation, and state whether or not he had read it. After

Ochs had read and explained to him the 64th Article of War, he again remained silent when asked if he understood the gravity of the offense he would commit if he refused to obey the order of his commanding officer. Capt. Chiappe again ordered him to read the regulation and to state whether or not he understood it. Colbert still remained silent even when asked whether he refused to state whether he had read it. Colbert was charged with willful disobedience of Chiappe's order to state if he had read the regulation.

Two officers made brief statements at the investigation of the charges against them. 2nd Lt. Argonne F. Harding said that he "did not think that all the witnesses named were present during his interview with Capt. Ochs." 2nd Lt. Victor L. Ransom stated that he had believed "he had been appearing before a board of officers at his interview, and should have been informed of his rights under the 24th Article of War, which was not read." He further said at the investigation that he "did not believe that he had been given the opportunity to sign a separate endorsement personally prepared by him to the effect that he had read Base Regulation 85-2." The witnesses in Ransom's case all agreed that he was correct in this respect, and amended their statements of expected testimony accordingly.[27]

Nevertheless, those of us who had been arrested felt that many officers had simply signed the regulation. Selway's testimony given at Freeman Field on April 16, 1945, stated "that a few of the trainee officers signed it as written, some signed it striking out the words 'and fully understand.' Others signed it, but wrote endorsements claiming that it was racial discrimination." Selway's comments corroborate the feelings of the arrested officers.

The 619th Also Has Problems

Many of the officers of the 619th Bombardment Squadron expressed their unwillingness to sign the prepared endorsement written on the reverse side of the regulation. Maj. John B. Tyson, their commander, advised them that they could merely certify that they had read the regulation. They could also delete any of the words on the prepared endorsement, or they could prepare their own endorsement. This self-written endorsement should say that they had read the regulation. Additionally, they should state their reasons for not being able to understand it. Nineteen lieutenants and flight officers of the 619th refused to certify in any manner that they had read Base Regulation 85-2.

On April 11, 1945, the officers of the 619th Bombardment Squadron who had refused to certify they had read 85-2 were called before the same board that had interviewed us. The officer or flight officer concerned was requested to state whether he had read the regulation in question. Seventeen replied that they had read it, and one of them read it only when told to do so. Another officer, 1st Lt. Arthur L. Ward, would not read it when told to do so. He replied "I have nothing to say," when given a direct order by Maj. Tyson to read the regulation. He remained silent.

Each officer, including Lt. Ward, was requested to state whether he would be willing to certify voluntarily over his signature that he had read Base Regulation 85-2. The officer would do so by signing the prepared endorsement with the words, "and fully understand," deleted from the statement. The officer could sign a statement prepared by himself that he had read it. Each of these 19 officers and flight officers expressed or indicated his unwillingness to certify. Capt. Ochs then read to each officer concerned the 64th Article of War, and fully explained the provisions thereof. He asked each accused if he understood the gravity of the offense, disobeying a direct order of his commanding officer in time of war. Each officer (except Lt. Ward, who remained silent) replied that he understood the seriousness of such an offense. Then, at the suggestion of Ochs, Tyson gave a direct order to the particular officer being interviewed. Tyson addressed each officer by name, in the following words: "I, as your Commanding Officer, order you to certify over your signature that you have read Base Regulation 85-2." With the exception of Ward, each officer refused to obey Tyson's order. Ward, after having been advised of the seriousness of such an offense by Ochs, replied, "I have nothing to say." When asked by Tyson if he refused to read the Base Regulation, he gave the same reply.

1st Lt. James B. Williams said that at no time did he refuse to sign Base Regulation 85-2. He had lost or misplaced his copy of the regulation, and had requested another one from Tyson, but had been unable to obtain it. In reply to this statement, Tyson admitted that Williams had said on April 10, 1945, that he had lost his copy; however, Williams was given another copy on the following day, and refused to sign it. Additionally, other comments made by officers who had not signed were either that they had not been given the opportunity to sign a separate endorsement prepared personally by themselves, or an endorsement with the words "fully understand" deleted.[28]

Endorsement

Many officers did sign separate endorsements, however. Many of these endorsements were very powerful and moving. All were very intense and well written. The following are examples:

The undersigned felt, and feels, that to have signed an endorsement signifying that he understood the regulation in question, as required by Paragraph 8 therein, would have constituted a false official statement inasmuch as the undersigned did not and does not understand the cited regulation. Such an act would not only have in itself rendered the undersigned liable to trial and punishment by a general court-martial, it would have done violence to the conscience of the undersigned; it would have constituted moral conduct less than that required of an officer and gentlemen in the Army of the United States. To have signed a statement to the effect would have been to tell a half truth and certainly would not have affected compliance with the written order contained in Paragraph 6 of the cited regulation. Such an act would have constituted moral "weaseling" and would have been no less contemptible, or dishonest, than to have signed the statement in full. To have affixed a signature to the document with further comment would have been equally dishonest.

Had this been a game in bullshit throwing, this one would have hit a home run and put the game out of reach of the opponents.

The undersigned could not, and cannot, understand how a medical officer qualified as a flight surgeon, having completed years of private medical practice and having completed all required Army medical training, could have been classified as "trainee" personnel, unless the distinction were solely one of color.

The undersigned could not, and does not, understand how the requirements of separate curfew referred to in Paragraphs 1 and 2 of the cited regulation could extend to tennis courts, usable only in daylight, and obviously affected by no curfew, unless the differentiation is purely "Jim Crow" in nature.

For the record, the undersigned wishes to indicate over his signature his unshakable belief that racial bias is Fascistic, un-American, and directly contrary to the ideals for which he is willing to fight and die. There is no officer in the army who is willing to fight harder, or more honorably, for his county and the command than the undersigned, nor is there an officer with a deeper respect for the lawful orders of superior authority. The undersigned does not expect or request any preferential treatment for the render of this service, but asks only protection of his submittal rights as a soldier and as an individual, the same identical opportunities for service and advancement offered all other military personnel, and the extension of the identical courtesies extended to all other officers of the Army.[29]

These statements are but a few that were cited in the report submitted by the board.

Signing a personal endorsement was an alternative provided by Selway. It was not one of our objectives. Our sole objective was to refuse to sign any statement whatsoever in conjunction with Base Regulation 85-2. I would suspect that many of these additional statements were written by the more senior officers who would have been looking to protect their careers.

Was This Mutiny?

Maj. Osborne was out to score big with Gen. Hunter. In addition to finding in his investigation that the 101 officers and flight officers were chargeable under the 64th article of War, he wanted to add mutiny to the charge. He stated in his report that when the officers and flight officers of the 619th Bombardment Squadron who had persisted, on April 11, in refusing to certify that they had read the regulation, they should also be charged with having joined in a mutiny on April 10. He felt that mutiny had been committed when they concretely refused, at the meeting of the officers of their organization, to obey the order of Maj. Tyson, their Commanding Officer, to execute certificates that they had read the regulation. The disobedience of the officers of an order given each one of them separately by Tyson on the following day "not only is properly chargeable as a violation to the 64th

Article of War, but is properly considered as evidence of the previous mutinous intent of each one. This mutinous intent persisted even after every effort was made to dissuade them from committing the offense." He used the same reasoning in the charge of mutiny against the members of Squadron E, 118th AAF, Base Unit who refused to sign Base Regulation 85-2.

Was There a "Mole" Within the Group?

The most definitive information with reference to spying by black officers comes from a telephone conversation between Selway and Gen. Glenn immediately after the first of us had been arrested at Officers Club Number Two. Selway was pleased to report that he had access to inside information: "The evidence I got this morning is apparently from one colored officer who was with them down at Godman Field before they combined the CCTS program at Freeman. The train came in yesterday..."

Glenn was very interested, and interrupted Selway's detailed account. "What was his name?" he asked.

"Silvera, " Selway replied, "and he's the one who is trying to give proof of loyalty because I fooled him a couple of times before, and he's a little scared. He told Captain Pughsley, that's another colored officer, Executive Officer of the 616th, that this had been organized in advance, essentially organized at Godman Field, and that they came up here prepared to do this in an organized manner."

At the same time, Selway claimed he had a second source. He told Glenn, "Now, another officer... I haven't gotten his name... told Captain Chiappe that he went down with the 33 because the rest had threatened him, and he was scared to go overseas with them if he didn't go along with the rest of the Negroes..."

It is possible that Selway's references to spies are without foundation. His claims have never been substantiated by any black officer. Nevertheless, this dark page in the history of the mutiny is a part of the official record, and must be addressed.

The telephone call to Maj. Murphy on April 5 by a black officer, revealing our planned entry into the Club, was only the first. In addition, Selway revealed that "at approximately 1945 hours on April 13, 1945, while I was at dinner at the mess, I received a call from one of the trainee officers. This officer stated that the trainees were forming up 100 percent in their quarters area, and that they were coming to Club Number Two to force entrance and create an incident. He further stated that they had announced that they want the program canceled. He stated that it was necessary for him to get back in the crowd and away from this telephone quickly because if they discovered him, and if he did not accompany them, it would be too bad for him. He said that they were angry at the few colored officers who had flown that day, and that the mass of the officers wanted the airplanes grounded and the precipitation of a mass incident which would result in a mass arrest and a mass trial."

When Selway told Hunter that colored officers were telling him things, I wanted this statement to be a lie. I wanted a reason to believe that this was a fabrication on his part. Nevertheless, after reading the remaining pages of his testimony and his statements in a telephone conversation with Hunter, where he concluded the conversation by informing Hunter that "spies within the Negro units were keeping him informed," I realize a case can be made for the validity of his claims.[30]

Reports of telephone calls by black officers to the white authorities is strong evidence that some persons in the group were seeking a preferred position for themselves at the expenses of other members of the group. During the period of the mutiny itself, and the subsequent fallout, there were rumors of a mole in the group. Initially, this idea was dismissed as being a rumor started by the whites in hope of creating dissension within our group; yet, as time went on, with additional evaluation of Selway's statement, there seems to be valid evidence that this could have been true.

6

First Air Force Gets a Message

Faced with the impressive courage of 101 young black airmen, the chain of command began to crumble. Hunter had lost faith in Selway's ability to handle the situation in a manner that would maintain the segregation Hunter felt was so important, and, at the same time, would not get him and his command in trouble. He was feeling the heat, and it was time to place the blame on someone else. On April 10, 1945, he called Maj. Gen. Lawrence S. Kuter, the Assistant Chief of Staff for Plans, Headquarters Army Air Forces, to set his plan in motion. Hunter began, "I understand that Barney was going to talk to Gen. George C. Marshall, the Army Chief of Staff, about the colored trouble I've been having out at Freeman."

Gen. Kuter, seemingly reluctant to talk with Hunter, replied, "He expects to do that either today or tomorrow morning."

Hunter felt the negative reaction, but wanted to plead his case immediately. He stated, "I hope he doesn't talk about it until he knows more about it."

Kuter assured him, "He will not."

Nonetheless, Hunter began to state his case, and, at the same time, he began to put the blame on Selway. "Well, here's the dope. I sent General Haynes out there, and my Air Inspector, and my Provost Marshal, and one of my JAs. It looks like Selway handled things very poorly. He had no order out, he had an assignment of building order, that these people had never seen, so we released them all. There was no question but what this thing was planned, because they all went busting over there. It was organized, but we had nothing on them, except..."

Gen. Kuter interrupted, "...you could try them on?"

"None, except three of them who pushed by the Officer of the Day or the Provost Marshal, or whoever it was, and they pushed him aside physically. Now, those three we're going to try."

Hunter continued to unload responsibility. "Selway was picked by me to command the 477th. In fact, his selection was a bit irregular. I've delayed changing him—the colored thought they'd gotten Bill Boyd, and gotten two or three other officers I had to remove. I hated to change him. Based on information that I got down at your place the other day, I think I've got to make a change. Here's what I want to do, Larry. In the past, based on Selway's recommendations, I had him as the Base Commander and the Group Commander. What I want Barney to do is to get to Personnel and tell them they've got to find me an officer to command the base—a hand-picked officer. I will find a hand-picked Group Commander from my Medium Bombardment show to go out and command the group."

There is no doubt that Hunter wanted to make sure that Selway would take the blame for the "mess" at Freeman. He was ready to dump Selway, and was setting the machinery in motion. He knew that he was talking with a sympathetic friend in high places.

After a short pause to take this all in, Kuter replied as expected, "O.K. You would prefer to have the Base Commander picked here, is that right, Monk?"

"Well, I want to O.K. it, but I just haven't got anybody here. I haven't gotten very much selection. Now somebody did get me Guy Kirksey for Walterboro, hand picked, and he doesn't cause any trouble and he does sit on the lid. I have got a good deputy down there now, a young Texan, who is handling them perfectly right now at Walterboro, and has improved that place 100 percent in handling the blacks, and in every other respect. I want to find some good older officer, regular army, that can sit on the lid—a strong guy that knows how to command. *(Things were in worse shape at Walterboro than at Freeman.)* Selway is vacillating and weak, and he's so scared he's going to get in trouble, like Boyd, or get a reprimand that he doesn't know what to do. He's going to get a very poor efficiency report out of me, although I know it's a difficult thing, but I think he's handled it poorly." Hunter then turned to specifics: "Now, if you can spare a little time, I think I might read to you this order I had them publish. I'll send it down to you. *Hunter took credit for Base Regulation 85-2.*

"I'll acknowledge that this thing is written up a little more binding because I don't want them forcing their way in and starting a fight. If anything starts out there, there's a great many more colored than there are white, so that's why I had that put in there to try to keep them from going in those buildings unless they had permission from definite people. Now, in a white place you wouldn't have that in there, but I'm trying to avoid bloodshed and riot. But I did get a ruling from Army Air Forces that it was done at many stations, and that they agreed with it and backed it up."

When Hunter was faced with the need to defend his logic he reverted to the old timeworn "saw" used by all racists—they evoked the specter of violence. Hunter knew that we were a very disciplined group, although he would never admit it. He knew that we had no intentions of getting involved in any type of violence. In fact, on several occasions

Hunter had convinced Selway there would be no violence. When confronted with the emerging militancy of the black officers, Hunter began to rationalize that it would be easier to train the group if he maintained the old status quo of segregation. This rationalization blurred his discipline. He began to disguise real reasons with spurious reasons. The more he was attacked, the greater the smoke screen he continued to send out.

This smoke screen became a dodge from the real issue under consideration. Hunter continued to hide his real desire to destroy the 477th time and time again. He defended his policies with as many excuses and false premises and false standards as he could devise. He blamed the mutiny on every possible organization and person he could identify. The harder Hunter tried to convince Gen. Kuter, the more Kuter probed in the opposite direction.

Kuter stated, "I understand that it is legal and is completely supportable, but I'm thinking more of the public relations aspect than the legal aspect."

Hunter continued, "Well, I'll look into my bases. I can't do it at all bases because I don't have dual facilities at many bases."

Kuter agreed, "That's right. Well, this would be an Air Force policy which..."

Hunter interrupted again, "They told me that this was in vogue at a lot of places and was very desirable where they could do it, where they had facilities to keep the trainees separate from the others."

In a rush to get this conversation over with, Kuter gave tentative agreement, but added some additional comments that did not help Hunter's sagging spirits: "All right. Your telephone conversations with Ray Owens during this uproar at Freeman have been made a matter of record, and we have posted Barney on developments as you have reported them. Barney and all the rest of us are thoroughly satisfied with the way this disturbance has been handled, and you are supported in every action you're taking. I'd like to have you know that."

Hunter, seemingly without having heard what Kuter said, continued to make excuses for the situation he had gotten the Air Force into. "I know that the Air Force has been backing them, and I also know that they're in a difficult position, and I don't want to make it any more difficult for them. I try to avoid putting the Air Force in an embarrassing position. Now, I had to get out something or they were going to keep on charging into that club to force an issue. That's why I had Selway publish this order yesterday. He didn't have any order.

"Things have quieted down. They've been very orderly, but when I had all my people out there, and tried to question them, they took advantage of the 24th Article of War and refused to answer any question so you can't get anywhere." *(That was our plan.)*

Gen. Kuter, knowing the racial feeling of Hunter, hooked him again without Hunter's getting it.

"Well, I don't know any better people in the world to handle that sort of thing than you and CV."

Hunter chimed in with, "Well, I don't get excited at all, and I don't let them talk any colored. They don't mention race. I go out there and I don't discuss race, or anything to do with race. I tell them they're part of my show, and I'm trying to train them, and that's been my attitude all along."

At that point, Hunter got in a little bragging, which always seems to help when you are facing the hangman. Again, Hunter had misinterpreted what had been said. He thought that Gen. Kuter had given him a compliment. What Kuter actually had implied was that two racists like he and Vice Commander Gen. Owens were the best men to handle something like this. Likewise, it was further evidence that Hunter's vision of the real world had been blurred by his rationalization.

Kuter finished the conversation with the statement, "I think you're doing it well, Monk."[31]

Hunter didn't suspect a thing as he hung up the telephone. He reviewed the conversation just concluded with Kuter with mixed feelings. Meanwhile, he had not evaluated with any accuracy the degree of resistance by the black officers to his plan, and little did he know that there was a big surprise coming up.

The Signing

The next day, April 11, 1945, the TJA began calling us in for the interviews with the purpose of ordering us to sign their newly-minted Base Regulation 85-2, and it was telephone time again. Early in the day, someone from Freeman Field had already been on the telephone to Hunter, and had given him a hint of what was going on. Hunter hurried to get the news to the Deputy Chief of Staff Air Force, Brig. Gen. Ray Owens, although Hunter did not have much real information.

As soon as he got Gen. Owens on the telephone, Hunter burst out, "I've got a little more excitement at Freeman Field. They're all organized and banded together out there. Here's what's happened. Did you get the copy of that order we got out? It's on the way to you, marked attention of General Kuter. I read it to Kuter on telephone."

Bored, Owens answered, "I haven't seen a copy of it yet."

Hunter said, "I told Selway to get each one to initial it that he had read it and understood it. They have refused to read it. So, he's getting them in one at a time with four witnesses, and gives them an order to read it, directs them to read it, and they refuse, and then he orders them to read it. Then he reads the 64th Article of War to them again, and they still refuse to read it. They refuse to read an order. Then when each one refuses, he puts them in arrest in quarters, and is going to prefer charges against them."

"How many of them?" asked Owens.

"Only 22 have gone by so far, but he's still getting them in."

"And all of them refuse?" Owens asked incredulously.

"All of them refuse. They refuse to read the order when they're given a direct order to read it, and he's got stenographers in there taking it all down, and he's got colored and white officers as witnesses in there."

Owens listened and remarked, "Looks to me like he needs a *****" *(There is a blank and only these five asterisks in the official transcript. I wish I knew what he had said. The transcriber missed or omitted this part of his reply, but it is not hard to guess that the remark was not a favorable one for our side.)*

Hunter surmised, somewhat wistfully, "Well, I don't know, they won't let me do that, but they'd better back me up on this because they're banded together, and I hope I can get some charges on them of conspiracy, and so forth."

Hunter, it seems, was becoming seriously angry and frustrated.

Owens didn't share Hunter's enthusiasm on this exciting subject. "I'll tell Kuter about that, and I'll check to see if he's gotten your order yet."

"It was sent to you. He asked me to send it to you, and I put attention Gen. Kuter on the inside," replied Hunter, a bit puzzled.

"It hasn't come in yet. That's too bad."

"Well, now, if we can get them, we've got to teach them they're in the Army. And Secretary Stimson says, by George, that I wouldn't bend over backward. Instead of bending over backward to treat them fairly... I'm not bending over backward... I'm treating them in a straight military manner. If I had white troops doing that, I wouldn't."

"You would even do as much or more."[32]

The following day, Hunter telephoned Selway because "those colored," as he put it, had once again surprised him. This time, Hunter was very upset. He was not a happy camper, to put it mildly. "Now, I understood from a report yesterday from Colonel Wold, my Air Inspector, that you had these people in and were giving them orders to read this order, and they had refused. I understand now that you didn't do it, that you passed it on down to some Captain. Is that correct?"

Selway had no choice; he had to defend himself. "To each Squadron Commander. I had 425 of them..."

Almost immediately he was cut off by Hunter. "Well, the Squadron Commander was a witness there, but didn't you have your legal officer..."

This time, Selway wasted no time, and he leaped in. "The Squadron Commander, as their immediate Commander, gives them a direct order. There are two white officers there as witnesses, and two colored officers as witnesses. The Legal Officer reads the 64th Article of War and explains it to them before they give them the direct order, the secretary recording every word of it."

"Were you there?" asked Hunter, still not satisfied.

"I stepped in there. I got the mass of them off without having to give it as a direct order to them. I got signatures of 425, so there will probably be 150—that's my guess—that willfully will disobey a direct order that tells them to read and sign they have read. And we've got to go through with this, General. We can't pull any punches."

Hunter is beginning to realize that Selway is doing the best he can under the circumstances. "I don't want to pull any punches, that's just what I'm trying not to do. Are they going to try to get out by saying that they wouldn't sign… that they understood it?" asked Hunter.

"No, it's explained to them right there that they do not have to say they understand it, but they're getting a direct order from the squadron commanders that they will read and certify they have read it. They stand right up there and admit, 'I have read; I will not sign that I have read.' According to the 64th Article of War, it's willful disobedience of a direct order to them."

"All right." replied Hunter.

At this point, an exchange that is almost humorous begins. These senior officers start playing "tough guy" on discipline, but, instead of showing toughness, the dialogue sounds more like a couple of junior second lieutenants talking.

"If we're going to have any discipline in this Army…" Selway surmised.

"I'm the one that wants the discipline," interrupted Hunter.

"If we run on this, we might as well quit, General."

"I know that, I don't run on anything. I have no idea of running, but I want things done carefully so that we've got a position in Washington. Washington has been advised of everything that happens daily… top side in Washington… and they are backing me up and approving everything that's been done so far."

It is becoming ever more apparent to the two that their problem will not be able to be explained away as easily as they had thought. Selway began again to give some explanation, but again was cut off in mid-sentence while Hunter cast about for additional charges.

"The order has to do… it's not a mass thing, they're brought in as individuals," Selway added.

"Yes, but there is considered action on the thing, and that's an aspect I want your legal officer to look into, and I'll get my people to look hard at it to see if we can't get them under some form of conspiracy to be insubordinate, or whatever it is," said Hunter.

Selway still could not accept the fact that black officers had organized an operation of this scope alone. He honestly could not believe that we could be that far ahead of him on every move without some outside help. When, to his dismay, Selway realized that he was being confronted by articulate blacks with advanced black consciousness, he became angry and bewildered.

"How many of them have you got that refused point-blank to sign it?" inquired Hunter.

"About 60, so far. We've got 100 to process today, and—it's your guess or mine—I imagine most of them have gotten instructions to refuse to obey the order. That's about 150, probably out of 425 so far. Everything else… the group is out here and they're flying, except a few members of the Bomb Group. In other words, it was all CCTS organized."

"One Squadron in the Group wasn't it?"

"One Squadron in the Bomb Group," replied Selway.

Hunter and Selway have looked at all aspects of this operation without finding a satisfactory answer as to what the group of officers will do next. They become concerned with violence as a last resort.

"Now, you don't sense any...this is all guardhouse lawyer stuff...you don't sense that you're going to have any violence, do you?"

"No, they're going to do this thing very darned legally."

"You aren't afraid of any violence?"

"Oh, no," replied Selway.

"All right. I keep Washington, the Deputy Commander of the Army Air Forces, advised daily of what goes on and what action I've taken, and what action I'm having you take," said Hunter.

"Well, I won't admit racial. A couple of them came in to see me, and they tried to talk me into..."

"No, it's plain military discipline," interrupted Hunter.

"It's plain military discipline, and it's based on training."

Here comes a good statement. Stop, look, and listen!

Hunter, with as much resolve as possible, muses, "And it doesn't make any difference whether they're colored or white. In fact, if it were white, they would have been handled a little more forcibly."

How about that? If they had been white, there would not have been a problem. They would not have been barred from the club in the first place. This instructor-trainee bullshit would not have come up.

"Well, you saw what happened to that colored WAC thing the other day. They went soft on it," joined in Selway.[33]

This casual remark about the "colored WAC thing" refers to a celebrated case of severe discrimination that had taken place at Fort Devens, Massachusetts, just weeks previously. Four black WACs were court-martialed and convicted on a similar charge of disobeying a superior officer. These WACs had been trained as medical technicians and sent to Lovell General Hospital at Fort Devens.

Walter H. Crandall, the Commander, said, "I don't want any black WACs as medical technicians around this hospital. I want them to do the dirty work." The WACs protested this action, and four were convicted on March 20. They were sentenced to one year at hard labor and dishonorable discharge.

The conviction was overturned as a result of a protest spearheaded by Dr. Mary McLeod Bethune, the only black member of the National Advisory Committee of the WAC. There was a tremendous outcry by the American public, including numerous black organizations, such as the Alpha Kappa Alpha Sorority, The California State Association of Colored Women, NAACP, and the John Brown Organization of America. On April 2, the reviewing authority declared the findings and sentence in the cases of Mary E. Green, Anne C. Morrison, Alice E. Young, and Johnny Murphy to be null and void, and directed that they be released from restriction and restored to duty.[34] That recent precedent makes Selway and Hunter's concern easy to understand.

Hunter returned to specific strategy: "I've got some undercover reports that your white officers are doing too darned much talking, and you've got to get them in and warn them, and advise them not to. They can not be talking about this incident—they've got to watch their conversation. They're evidently talking in the club, and elsewhere generally, disobeying regulations, discussing racial problems, and making derogatory remarks about the colored, and they're going to get smacked down. I want just as strict discipline there for whites as I do for colored, and you've got to straighten them out on that."

"I heard about that."

"Anybody that goes in the club, you can find they're discussing those things and making very derogatory remarks about the colored. You've got to get all of your commanders in and give orders to the white that they will not... they will refrain... that this thing is happening. Read them the Army Regulations and whatnot on it, and that they will make no derogatory remarks on race at all. They will make no remarks about race. They can talk about people, but not about race. Get me?" ordered Hunter.

Now what is that all about? It was another of his little tricks to cover the race factor at all cost.

"Yes, sir, I'll take care of that."

"All right, now finish up those people, and let me know what the outcome is."

"Here's what I planned to do... I have to do one job here at a time. When I've got them all through, which will be on into the night—we worked until eleven last night—then I've got all of them in arrest or a certification on a piece of paper that they have read it. Do you want me to open the Club tomorrow?"

"Your Club? Yes, absolutely."

"I'll get this finished tonight, and open that thing tomorrow and see if we're going to get any violations," affirmed Selway.

"All right. I've made up my mind that's all right. Now don't get mad, you want to keep quiet, but I want you to have military discipline—what I think would be a good idea to do, after your people have all done this thing, I think it would be a good idea to have a meeting of all of them and advise them that they have to obey orders in the Army, and even if they think the order is illegal, they still have to obey it. They can object to it after obeying it if they don't think it's legal."

I must give Selway credit. He kept trying to please his boss.

"Well, here's an angle on that thing. I've had several of the officers, of those who have actually signed it, up for different reason, and they tell me that they consider the opening of the wound all the time to them is kind of an insult."

"I know, but you can tell them that they aren't the ones who are opening it."

"And this gang that we'll have under arrest, they would rather have the thing a forgotten subject, so we won't be prying the wound all the time."

"I know, but you've got the thing there," said Hunter.

Selway replied, "They understand it. It's just this gang…"

Hunter interrupted, "Well, you're the Base Commander, and you've got to be forceful, and I would have preferred if you had been in there yourself and done this thing!"

Selway, finding some hidden courage, answered back, "I've got 425 black officers, and then I have to handle that whole flock as individual cases, and have to be signed, you know."

Hunter said, "I know it. All right, you keep us advised, and I want you to show forceful command there, but I don't want you getting excited. I want things handled quietly and forcibly."

"Okay," agreed Selway.

"All right."[35]

That was some telephone call! Hunter was angry with Selway and he let him know it. Although Selway tried to stand up for his position as best he could, he knew the ball game was over for him.

Hunter Tries the Pentagon Again

Following this conversation, Hunter needed to phone Gen. Kuter and explain the situation to him. Hunter did not feel comfortable with Kuter, and kept working to get his blessing in the form of a more forceful endorsement. He got right down to business as soon as Kuter answered. "Larry, there have been some 60-odd out of 400 or so that have read this order and refused to sign it, and refused to sign an endorsement that they had read it. They were given a direct order by their Squadron Commander, with witnesses and everything, and stenographers taking it down, and they refused to do it. We've got them in arrest and we've got some more to go— about 100-odd more today—to cover them all, and I don't know how many of those will refuse."

Kuter, though not happy with the situation, replied, "O.K."

Hunter did not miss the tone of Kuter's voice, so he switched to bashing the black press. "Now, the guy that evidently is behind all this is one Lowell M. Trice. He's a reporter from the *Indianapolis Recorder*, a colored newspaper. He tried to get on the post without credentials from the War Department Press Bureau, and he was very antagonistic and raised hell, and they won't let him on the post."

"Is he the individual who got on the post and was ejected on the day the first disturbance occurred?" asked Kuter.

"Yes, and he tried to get on the next day, and they wouldn't let him on. And this has been reported to the War Department Bureau of Public Relations. Now he is down in the town, evidently advising these people. In other words, I consider it encouraging these people to disobey orders and stir up revolt in the Army. I would like if you could get the FBI on him and see just what he is doing."

Hunter had returned to the idea that some outsider or group of outsiders must have been masterminding every action we took. He and his staff were dumbfounded that we were capable of putting up such effective, well-organized resistance.

"We'll undertake to do just that," Kuter replied. "For your further information, Monk, Ray Owens and I talked to Barney and Mr. Lovett *(Robert A. Lovett, Assistant Secretary of War for Air)* on the current upset last night. None of us can suggest any better procedure than that which you are following. We are concerned, however, over the order which is the subject of this discussion. It had not yet arrived in Ray Owens' hands last night. We realize that the military offense under which you are putting these birds in arrest is not affected by the contents of that order."

Kuter was telling Hunter that HQ AAF were not buying into Base Regulation 85-2. Yet HQ AAF would try to back him on the military offense that we were charged under. Basically he is telling Hunter that the order was worthless. That was not well received by Hunter. His response was a curt. "That's correct."

"It doesn't matter what the order says, the military offense still stands," added Kuter.

Hunter replied hopefully, "Well, before that order was published, the only thing we got was three of them, and we got those for forcibly pushing aside an officer performing his duty."

He sounded disappointed because he could not report a higher total of arrested officers. Because of this order he was upping the number, and hoped it would earn him a pat on the back, but it was not to be.

"But for this, you are now placing them under arrest…"

Hunter rushed in, "For refusing to take a direct order to endorse that thing that they have read it."

Kuter agreed, "Yeah, I understand, and our concern is that there should be no trials until we are assured that the order itself will stand."

"All right, but they're in arrest in quarters?"

"That's correct, and should stay that way. Mr. Lovett particularly realizes the fact that the final case will probably not be settled on the military aspect of signing or refusing to sign the statement that they have read this piece of paper, that the case probably will be settled on the contents of the piece of paper." *The fat just hit the fire, and Hunter knew it.*

Secretary Lovett was making clear to the upper echelons of the Army Air Forces that if a person disobeyed an illegal order, that person could not be punished, assuming it was later proved that the order was illegal. For Hunter, it meant that if the content of the Base Regulation 85-2 was proven illegal because it violated the provisions of Army Regulation 210-10, there was no case. We officers were betting on this fact from the beginning. We felt that any case that was brought against us would not stand. What was contained in Base Regulation 85-2 was clearly illegal to us.

Hunter would not give in. He was skating on very thin ice. He continued to fight a huge battle without a suitable weapon.

"Well, I know, but there are two different aspects. I cannot run anything in the Army if I have white or colored that refuse to obey an order, and I can't do anything when they do. So there are two aspects to this; one is the refusal to take a direct order and comply with it, and the other one is I'm trying to see... there is undoubtedly collusion and conspiracy... and I'm trying to see if we can't work up a case on that. It may be just circumstantial evidence, and may not be strong enough to prove in open court, before a court-martial, but I'm having that aspect looked into. But I have got them, I am quite sure, on refusal to obey an order—and a legal order."

Kuter tried to warn Hunter, but he wouldn't take the hint.

"Yes, but do not…" Kuter attempted to add a point, but was interrupted.

"I'm preferring charges. I will not have any court-martials until I hear further"

"All right, Sir. That's the point."

"But I will have charges preferred," Hunter assured Kuter.

"O.K. Thank you, Monk."

"All right, not at all."[36]

This last exchange explains why the case fell apart. Kuter tried to tell Hunter that his case would not really fly. However, Hunter felt that, no matter what the circumstances, when an order was given and not obeyed, he had a case under the 64th Article of War to court-martial the person who refused the order.

Hunter, his vision blurred by his racist feelings, succumbed to temptation. He again disguised real reasons with spurious reasons. Secretary Lovett understood the situation and knew that Hunter was attempting a strategy that was illegal under the current Army regulation. It would not take a rocket scientist, or a even first-year law student, to see how misguided his plan was.

The Plan to Move the 101 to Godman

Hunter remained unsatisfied with his situation, and was even more uneasy after this call to Gen. Kuter. As soon as he received additional information, he again called Kuter. This time, Kuter had Gen. Owens listening in. "Monk, both Ray and I are in on this conversation."

Hunter began, "Larry, they're finishing up getting those lads to endorse that they've read this order, about 3:30 this afternoon, and they estimate there will be about 105 that will refuse."

"Out of 400."

"It's about 700 or 800 on the post; it's all white and colored officers, we make them both do it. Now, Selway's recommended, and I approve it, there will be 105 stewing around there in arrest in quarters. He wants to, and I have approved it, move them over to Godman, pending... they'll prefer charges against them... and pending your turning me loose to court-martial them, send them over to Godman to get the rotten apples out of that barrel so they won't stir up any more trouble."

"Any objections to that, Ray?"

"No, I don't..."

Hunter rushed ahead, always thinking about violence.

"There's also more white over there at Fort Knox, the Army Tank Training Center near Godman Field, and if they do start any trouble, there are plenty of white there. Otherwise, if anything starts at all, I'm going to request a battalion of MPs to go into Freeman."

Kuter didn't think much about the battalion of MPs.

"The former action would appear to attract less adverse comment than the latter, in my opinion. You agree, Ray?"

Hunter was on a roll.

"I'm trying to avoid the latter."

Gen. Owens agreed with Kuter.

"Yes, we must avoid the latter if we can."

"I'm not going to do the latter until violence starts, or I'm sure of it," said Hunter.

"How will you move them, Monk?" asked Kuter.

"Well, I imagine they will move them by air. I don't know whether they will move them by air or train."

"It would be more desirable by air, wouldn't it?"

"Yes, but I haven't got the air transportation."

"The Troop Carrier could do that, couldn't it, Ray?"

"Yes, they could do it I am sure. They always have airplanes to do things like that."

"Ray, will you call Olds' headquarters and tell him to meet a request for air transportation for them from Freeman Field? And, Monk, will you have Freeman Field call Olds for such transportation as is needed? And do make the movement, and do make it by air."

"I will. Right."

Kuter asked, "Anything further?"

Hunter could never pass up a chance to get in more words, especially when he smelled a hint of cooperation from upper echelon people.

"No. Now, I'm preferring charges against all of those people for willful disobedience of a direct order, charging them under the 64th Article of War. As I say, I'm not doing any trying. I'm bringing down with me the charges against those three original ones. So, you can have your Judge Advocate General look them over, or anybody else that wants to. I'll be down there in the morning."[37]

The battle had heated up. Selway wanted to get us away from Freeman Field back to Godman Field while arranging our court-martial. He suggested this move to Hunter, who agreed with the idea and convinced Gen. Kuter to go along with the move. As a result, Selway felt much better. He had never been sure that the black officers would not become violent, and should a violent incident break out, he wanted white MPs available. With these officers at Godman Field, located just across from Fort Knox, the largest armored training base in the world, there would be hundreds of white MPs readily available.

Although we kept the power structure confused and upset, Selway tried to explain why we were acting as we were. "It's quite evident that they are displeased with the fact that the racial question has not entered into any of the investigation or charges or orders, and they are displeased with the fact that each question has been handled as an individual case and not as a mass. I am certain that… as sure as we were born… that upon opening of Officers Club Number Two, the Negro officers will move in en masse to continue their test and crusade to force investigation of segregation based on any reason at all. I do not have the legal staff or the white security troops to handle any such situation. I believe we would have to start all over again, charging them with breach of arrest or violation of this regulation governing housing. I don't have the personnel or the facilities to handle any such mass affair."

That was further evidence that Selway hadn't the vaguest idea of what we were thinking, a fact clear each time he began to talk about what the plans and desired results of our actions were. However, he was correct on one thing. If he had opened that club, there would have been many more black officers who would have gone in. He would have had to arrest all but a few of the officers stationed at Freeman Field.

Now that HQ AAF had agreed to move the arrestees back to Godman Field, Hunter wanted Selway to fill him in on a few details. "All right, who are you going to have in command at Godman?"

"I've got McDowell to command it."

"All right."

"All right, that's all right. I have no objection to your moving them to Godman," replied Hunter.

"At Godman, I think we have 20 white MPs and a Provost Marshal. That's sufficient to check them and secure them, and, since they would be right next to Fort Knox, we would not have to move in an MP battalion, or something, you see?" remarked Selway.

Selway then suggested that the commitment date of the two groups, bomb and service, be moved up. "Our present estimate is that all minimums for POM (Preparation for Overseas Movement) AAF Standards 220-1, and the changes thereto, can be met within six weeks except for the shortage of crews in the 619th Squadron, on the presumption that those officers in that squadron, now in arrest, will be convicted."

"Well, I can't do that. There's some stuff coming out pretty soon, I'll let you know. Army Air Forces is working on it. It's not going out early, I can guarantee you that."

Hunter was hoping that the program would be canceled!

"Well, the augmentation of the replacement program is, of course, postponed or collapsed here..."

"As soon as I can get definite information from Washington, I'm going to give it to you."

"O.K. Well, if I open tomorrow... can I wait until I move those people out anyway?"

"Yes, but I'd get them moved right away. Now, the only thing about moving them, how are you going to investigate the thing if you've got them over at Godman?"

"Well, there are only four people that... and the secretary and legal officer..."

"If you've got everything, and don't have to investigate them, I'd move them right away."

"I'll move them right away. I've got a festering sore and we might as well move it.

"O.K., move them out to Godman right away. I'm going down to Washington tomorrow and I'll talk to them. I approve your moving those 105."

"That's the estimated number it will be at 3:30." *They never did get the number right.*

"Well, whatever it is, move them to Godman until we decide what we're going to do with them. In arrest at Godman."

"All right, General. Thank you very much."[38]

The incredible amount of time and effort that these high-ranking officers of the Army Air Forces were taking in the middle of a general war, to ensure the continued segregation of black officers, was amazing. Hunter was far more dedicated to seeing his racist policies enforced than he was concerned with the training of the bomb group to fight the enemy.

We had no intentions of breaching arrest. We were confident that the fact that 104 of us were arrested would be sufficient to bring a public outcry that would rout Gen. Hunter. We had some hope, moreover that the large number of arrests might induce the War Department to act in a different way toward black Air Force officers.

The information about the planned transfer of the 477th Bombardment Group back to Godman Field leaked out and attracted the attention of Frank R. Beckwith, Chairman of the Committee on Legal and Legislative Affairs of the Federation of Associated Clubs. He sent a telegram to Congressman Louis Ludow from Indiana in which he requested that the Congressman intervene and, if possible, have the matter held in status quo until it was thoroughly investigated by the House Committee. This telegram was sent on April 29.

However, by the time the War Department got around to answering, it was too late. The response was short and vague: "In reply to your letter of April 30 and its enclosure requesting that the transfer of the 477th Bomb Group and its supporting units from Freeman Field be held up, I have been asked to inform you that this transfer already has been accomplished. As you know, an investigation of occurrences incident to the tour of duty of the 477th Bomb Group at Freeman Field, where these units were recently stationed, has been completed, and the Secretary intends to advise you of the results of War Department action on the recommendations submitted in the report of investigation as promptly as circumstances will permit."

One can only wonder what would have been the answer had this letter been received prior to the our movement from Freeman to Godman. Would it have made a difference? Would the movement have been canceled? I think not.

7

In Arrest At Godman

Word had spread across the base that the prisoners, 101 black officers, were being shipped off the station. A crowd of the base personnel, black and white, had rushed down to the flight line to observe. Included were a number of the black enlisted men who had given total support to the protest, as well as black officers from the Bomb Group. Of course, a majority of the white personnel was out on the ramp, merely for the show, to watch the transfer of the prisoners. Rumor had it that we were being shipped to the Army prison at Fort Leavenworth, Kansas, but Lt. Samuel Black, the tower Duty Officer that day, had signed the clearance, and knew that the destination was Godman Field. He would squash the rumor shortly after the aircraft took off.

When we arrived at the flight line, we were lined up on the tarmac. My eyes fixed on a tableau of unbelievable viciousness. I noticed a black enlisted airman photographer actively taking pictures with an official camera. Suddenly, a white officer approached him and demanded the camera. The black sergeant very slowly handed over the government-issued camera. As it neared the white officer's hand, he snatched it away. With an angry sneer on his face, he unloaded it and removed the film, exposing it. He then threw the film on the ground, and, with a slow, deliberate grinding motion, crushed it under his foot. This officer repeated this inexcusable act involving another black cameraman. I was filled with revulsion and disgust at the pettiness and length that these people were going in their effort to humiliate us. More regrettably, I feared this historic and important event in history would go unverified and unrecorded.

However, the April 28, 1945, issue of the *Pittsburgh Courier* featured a photograph of our group standing on the ramp on the front page. I did not know how this photograph was taken, or how it made the front page of the *Courier*. I found the answers in 1970, when I met M/Sgt. Harold J. Beaulieu, Sr., at Travis Air Force Base, California. In April 1945, he had been the non-commissioned officer in charge of the photo lab at Freeman Field. On that fateful morning he had a gut feeling that the white hierarchy would not want the event recorded. He rigged up a camera in a shoe box, and, after strategically positioning himself, he took the photo that appeared in the *Courier*. Once again, a black man had demonstrated his resiliency and ability to outsmart his adversary in times of turmoil.

We stood on the edge of the runway waiting to board these aircraft without a clue as to where we were going. After approximately 30 minutes, we were loaded aboard the aircraft. One hundred and one United States Army Air Forces officers under arrest! We did not talk about what was happening. We kept our deep thoughts to ourselves and our conversation lighthearted.

The transports moved out. We still were not told our destination even after we were aboard. We could only guess. During the first few moments after takeoff, we continued to speculate on our destination. As aviators who had frequently flown over the territory, we felt that by looking out at the ground we should be able to identify certain landmarks, thereby fixing our position and our route of flight. It became evident from the direction of the sun relative to our line of flight that we were flying in a southerly direction, and very shortly after takeoff we crossed the Ohio River. Having crossed this easily identifiable landmark, the aircraft began to descend in preparation for landing. These actions and the short time required for the flight made clear to us that we were returning to Godman Field, an air base from which we had departed only eight days previous.

We landed at Godman Field. As we looked out of the aircraft, there on the ramp were parked several large prison transport vans. The primary use of these vans was to transport the German and Italian prisoners of war at the POW camp located there at Fort Knox. In front of these vehicles, standing in rigid formation, were approximately 75 Military Police armed with sub-machine guns. We disembarked and were herded aboard these vans. We were being transported just as if we were prisoners of war. The German POWs, walking around without guards, were laughing at us.

We could not in our wildest imagination believe that a group of United States Army Air Force officers were being treated in this manner. Within a few minutes after departing the flight line, we arrived at the Officers Quarters area, the same place that had been home to our group only a few short days ago. This area contained four wooden, two-story buildings, with a single-story mess building in the middle. We disembarked from these hated vans and went inside the barracks. We were " home" again, but this time we did not know how long we would remain there.

When we arrived, Army engineers and construction personnel were busy installing lights on light poles around the area. There were plans to include barbed wire as an added insult, but that project was never completed. A young white private was walking around with an MP band on his arm, and carrying a billy club. A fellow arrestee, and my roomate,

2nd Lt. Robert B. Johnson, walked over and asked the soldier what he was going to do with that billy club. The soldier saluted, looked embarrassed, and said, "I don't know, Sir. I don't even know why I'm here."

The Base Commander had opened the officers mess, and, in addition to reactivating the dining facility, a small post exchange had been set up and stocked with the barest of necessities. Clearly, they were planning a long stay for us. They knew that it would take a long while to court-martial such a large group.

As we settled in, we also were looking forward to a long stay, and began to plan for day-to-day operations under semi-field conditions. We were isolated from the normal air base and were being held incommunicado. Authorities had no intention to make us available to the public. We would not as a group, nor as individuals, talk about our plans while inside the barracks. We suspected that the command had bugged the barracks, and that anything we said would be immediately revealed to Gen. Hunter. Consequently, we would meet in small groups at night outside our barracks to discuss what our next moves would be. The major topic of most discussions was what our responses would be to questions that would be posed to us by the Selway people.

On April 16, a team of officers and legal clerks from First Air Force and Freeman Field arrived at Godman Field. They were there to begin processing court-martial charges against each of the 101. Two days later, a team of officers from HQ AAF Inspector General's Office, led by Lt. Col. Smith W. Brookhart, Jr., and including Col. J. A. Hunt and Lt. Grant P. Hall, arrived at Godman Field. They were there to conduct a high-level investigation into our case. This team of inspectors interviewed all the arrested officers.

During my interview with Col. Hunt, I was aware that he was trying to find out exactly what had taken place at Freeman Field on April 5 and 6, 1945. After I had talked for several minutes with Hunt, he instructed the secretary to turn off the recorder. He then asked, "Flight Officer Warren, will you tell me, off the record, just what you think is the problem?" I looked at the Colonel for a long moment. Could I trust him with the truth? It then occurred to me, what harm could I do by telling him how I really felt? Would it really matter whether I trusted him or not? Regardless, here was a chance to tell a Colonel from the Pentagon what I thought about the situation. I did not have high hopes of making a great impression, but I accepted the opportunity to speak my mind.

I began in a slow and deliberate manner, I said, "I do not believe that we should be fighting this war to preserve democracy and freedom in segregated groups. Nor should we be labeled a black Bomber Group when all the command positions are held by whites. Should we go to combat so structured and perform outstandingly, the performance would be attributed to the brilliant leadership of the white officers. On the other hand, should the performance be less than outstanding, the performance would be attributed to the fact that we were an all-black outfit. If we must serve in a segregated unit, it must be a black unit from the Commander to the lowest-ranking person in the group."

The clubs at Freeman Field remained closed. We at Godman Field were under arrest, with no assignments, and with only time on our hands. We spent most of our time playing bridge and pinochle. F/O Ario Dixione—ever looking for a way to turn a buck—hand-made some bingo cards and ran a nightly bingo game. 2nd Lt. Silas M. Jenkins was appointed the supply, mess and other duties officer. He was in charge of the dining hall and the very small PX that supplied us with the bare necessities. He did an excellent job. We ate well.

It was at this time that President Franklin D. Roosevelt, a strong supporter of blacks in Army aviation, died at Warm Springs, Georgia. Vice President Harry S. Truman became President. Many of us were unaware of the influence that Senator Truman played in enabling blacks to participate in the Civilian Pilot Training Program, and we viewed his succession to the Presidency with doubts and misgivings. These misgivings, of course, later proved to be without foundation.

Subsequently, authorities moved Bill Terry, Marsden Thompson, and Shirley Clinton from Freeman Field to Godman Field, but we could not talk to them. They were isolated from our group. However, we could wave or yell a greeting to them when we would see them being escorted to the dining facility.

Selway had ordered us not to attempt to communicate with the outside world. Nevertheless, we were able to get messages out to the press and other important persons. There are stories of the many methods we used to get these messages out. Some were simply fantasy, but most were true. One of the most romantic, yet unsubstantiated, was that girlfriends would drive by in convertibles, and someone would throw the message into the open car from the upper story of the barracks. Specifically, any messages for the outside world were passed to operators who had slipped into the area under the cover of darkness. Security was very lax. The messages that we passed to these people went directly to the addressees. On the other hand, all the information that was needed for the outside world was known by the person-nel who remained at Freeman Field. They knew how to get out the information and to whom. Lt. Weldon "Bootie" Green, a newspaper reporter in civilian life, was told to sign the regulation so he would not be arrested and could act as our liaison to the press. Many of us told him, "Bootie! You go in there and sign anything. Just don't get arrested."

After the Air Forces Inspector General's visit to Godman, our daily activities settled into a regular routine. Several days passed, and then it was almost as if you could feel the tension. The air was electric with anticipation as the rumors began to fly. The hottest rumor was that we were going to be released soon, and that Col. Benjamin O. Davis, Jr., the highest ranking black officer in the USAAF, would be taking over as Group Commander. We especially hoped that this rumor was true. So we waited.

I had never seen morale so high in a group of men who were under such great stress. We were proud of what we had done, and how we were doing it. We had faced the problem as strong black men should. We thought we had a chance of winning. Now, we were sure that we would win. We knew that what we were doing would not completely remove segregation from all the armed forces, but maybe the 477th Bomb Group could be the start.

Our greatest wish and desire was to get back to Freeman Field and complete our combat training. We wanted to get overseas, and prove that we could fight in bombing aircraft as well as the 332nd Fighter Group had proved that blacks could fight in fighter aircraft.

8

The Nation and Congress Get Involved

Irate American citizens flooded the War Department with more than 50,000 telegrams and letters protesting the arrest of 104 black officers. At the same time, thousands of letters poured into the offices of the Congress and to the office of President Roosevelt.

One such letter, addressed to Senator Scott Lucas of Illinois, was one of the strongest letters sent to the Congress. It was from Edwin Johnson, the Legislative Director of Lodge 748 of the International Workers. "The recent arrest and removal by the Army of Negro Flight Officer Trainees at Freeman Field for refusing to sign away their rights as citizens is in direct violation of an order forbidding discrimination against Negroes in any army camp. It also serves to demoralize these Negro servicemen, instead of building up their morale, making them feel that they have something to fight for. It is regrettable that such a thing could happen in the United States at this time. The ones who should have been arrested are those who tried to make them sign this undemocratic, discriminatory guarantee—it goes against everything democratic and liberal, it goes against all principles and fair play. It smacks more of the way our enemies treat their minorities. We want to protest most vigorously against such undemocratic and discriminatory practice in the armed forces of the United States.

"We hope sir, that you will take immediate steps to remedy this injustice; to see that they be reinstated at their former posts at Freeman Field, and that the white officers be punished for their unlawful acts."

This letter was only one of many examples of correspondence sent to the War Department from congressional representatives. An impressive list of Congressmen and national leaders became involved in the protest of the actions being taken by the Air Force. Many of these persons were acting on their own; others were responding to inquiries by their constituents.

Edith Terry, the mother of Roger Terry, was not a person to sit idly by while her son was under arrest, especially since she was well connected politically. She sent a telegram to Congressman Vito Marcantonio of New York requesting information in reference to her son. Numerous other law-makers, who had heard about the situation, made inquiries. All wanted to know what was going on at Freeman Field.

One of the most influential non-government communications was from Walter White the Secretary of the NAACP. He sent the following telegram to President Roosevelt. Unfortunately President Roosevelt died the following day:

W541 LG PAID NEW YORK
   WUX NY APR 11 1945 138P
PRESIDENT FRANKLIN D ROOSEVELT
THE WHITE HOUSE
NATIONAL ASSOCIATION FOR THE ADVANCEMENT OF COL-
ORED PEOPLE IS ADVISED 58 MEN OF THE 118TH ARMY AIR
FORCE BASE UNIT AT FREEMAN FIELD, INDIANA, ARE UNDER
ARREST ALLEGEDLY FOR ENTERING AN OFFICERS CLUB SAID
TO BE RESERVED FOR WHITE OFFICERS ONLY. ARRESTED
MEN INCLUDE CAPTAINS, LIEUTENANTS AND FLIGHT OFFIC-
ERS, INCLUDING SEVERAL OVERSEAS VETERANS WHO HAVE
COMPLETED MISSIONS WITH 15TH AIR FORCE IN MEDITERRA-
NEAN. WE ARE FURTHER ADVISED THAT A TOTAL OF 90 MEN
HAVE SIGNIFIED THEIR WILLINGNESS TO RESIGN THEIR COM-
MISSIONS IF SEPARATE OFFICERS CLUBS ARE TO BE MAIN-

TAINED, ORDER BARRING NEGRO OFFICERS FROM CLUB, SAID TO HAVE BEEN ISSUED BY COLONEL ROBERT SELWAY, JR. WHO ISSUED AND ENFORCED SIMILAR ORDERS SELFRIDGE FIELD, MICHIGAN, IN 1943, WHEN SOME OF THE MEN NOW UNDER ARREST WERE COMPLETING THEIR FLIGHT TRAINING PREPARATORY TO ENTERING COMBAT SERVICE IN MEDITER-RANEAN. WE BELIEVE THIS ORDER IS IN VIOLATION OF ARMY MEMORANDUM ISSUED LAST AUGUST ABOLISHING DISCRIMI-NATION BASED ON RACE AT ARMY POSTS AND TRAINING FACILITIES, ALSO OF AR 210-10 PARAGRAPH 19. WE ARE SURE WE DO NOT NEED TO STRESS DEVASTATING EFFECT UPON CIVILIAN AND SOLDIER MORALE AMONG NEGRO AMERICANS OR THESE WHOLESALE ARRESTS. RECENT OCCURRENCES IN BOTH ARMY AND NAVY HAVE DEMONSTRATED DEEP RESENT-MENT OF COLORED PERSONNEL TO HUMILIATING SEGREGA-TION AND DISCRIMINATION BASED ON COLOR. ON THE OTHER HAND OFFICIAL REPORTS OF SUCCESSFUL INTEGRATION OF NEGRO RIFLE UNITS WITH WHITE COMRADES IN BATTLE OF GERMANY ON ORDER OF GENERALS EISENHOWER AND LEE INDICATE THAT POLICY OF NON-SEGREGATION WILL WORK IN BATTLE AND AT SAME TIME WILL IMPROVE MORALE OF NEGRO AND WHITE SOLDIERS. WE URGE PROMPT ACTION TO REVOKE COLONEL SELWAY'S ORDER, AND TO RELEASE OFFICERS FROM ARREST. RESPECTFULLY YOURS
WALTER WHITE SECRETARY.

Gen. Ulio, the Adjutant General of the Army, wrote the following reply:

Dear Mr. White:

Your telegram of 11 April 1945, addressed to the President, concerning conditions at Freeman Field, Seymour, Indiana, has been referred to the War Department for reply. An investigation is now being conducted at Freeman Field and you may be assured that if any corrective action is found to be necessary it will be taken.

Sincerely yours,

J. A. ULIO
Major General
The Adjutant General

A telegram from Congressman Adam Clayton Powell made clear his interest in the matter:

WAR V WU A161 51 GOVT 10 EXTRA BU WASHINGTON DC APR 16 1945 336P

HONORABLE HENRY L STIMSON

SECRETARY OF WAR WASH DC

WE URGE AN IMMEDIATE INVESTIGATION OF THE ENTIRE SITUATION AT FREEMAN AND GODMAN FIELD INDIANA INVOLVING RANK INJUSTICES FORCED UPON 101 NEGRO ARMY AIR FORCE OFFICERS. ALSO AN IMMEDIATE INVESTIGATION OF COLONEL ROBERT SELWAY COMMANDING OFFICER. A REPLY WILL BE APPRECIATED

ADAM CLAYTON POWELL JR 22ND DISTRICT NEW YORK EMANUEL CELLER 15TH DISTRICT NEW YORK[39]

The number of interested law makers was long, and the following is but a short list of these legislators:

Senator Scott Lucas, Illinois
Senator Raymond E Willis, Indiana
Senator E. Alexander Smith, New Jersey
Senator Francis J. Meyers, Pennsylvania
Senator Albert W. Hawkes, New Jersey
Senator Edwin C. Johnson, Colorado
Senator Homer Ferguson, Michigan
Senator Arthur H. Vandenberg, Michigan
Representative Adam Clayton Powell, New York
Representative Emanual Cellers, New York
Representative James Curley, Massachuetts
Representative George Bender, Ohio
Representative Louis Ludlow, Indiana
Representative William W. Link, Illinois
Representative William A. Rowan, Illinois
Representative Herbert J. McGlinchey, Pennsylvania
Representative John Edward Sheridan, Pennsylvania[40]

These letters required the War Department to develop a standard reply to these lawmakers and other interested persons. These replies ended with the final paragraph based on the time of the reply. If the reply was early during the period, it concluded with the following:

"A representative of the Office of the Air Inspector is now at Freeman Field engaged in a full investigation of all aspects of the subject incident. When the report of investigation is received in this Headquarters, complete information will be furnished."

If the request was received after we were sent to Godman, the reply would read thus:

"An investigation is now being conducted at Freeman Field, and you may be assured that if any corrective action is found to be necessary, it will be taken."[41]

Planning Our Defense

Meanwhile, we were planning our defense. We needed assistance from someone who had a good knowledge of the law, and, fortunately, there was a very good one available.

The story of how we were saved from our own folly has been documented in *The Tuskegee Airmen,* by Lt. Charles E. Francis: "2nd Lt. William T. Coleman, a law student from Philadelphia, sat alone and listened. While the talk subsided, he arose and said, 'I have been sitting here listening to a bunch of damn dummies planning how to get all of you hanged or sent to prison for life. Now if you don't know what you're doing, you'd better ask someone. You are not challenging a Colonel or a General, you're challenging the War Department and the United States Government. Believe me, they are just waiting for you to make one mistake—one mistake, and they will be on you like a bunch of tigers.' One of the officers sarcastically remarked, 'If this gentleman is so smart, smarter than all of us dummies, I am sure he will advise us as to what we should do to save our necks.' Another officer remarked, 'If you don't know it, he was a Philadelphia law student before entering the service. We all know that Philadelphia lawyers have a reputation for knowing everything about the law.' Anyway, Lt. Coleman replied, 'If you guys listen to me, and don't go too far, everything will be all right. So, don't worry, I'm going to get you out. Just follow my instructions. I will draft a letter, and I want each of you to copy the letter and submit your letter to the Commanding Officer at Freeman Field."[42]

We did not have a typewriter available, so each of us had to make our copy of the letter by hand. I still have my original copy, as Col. Selway returned each letter with his endorsement rejecting our demands because charges had not been filed at that time:

Subject: Request for Individual Counsel.

TO: Commanding Officer, Freeman Field, Ind.

I, being advised of my rights to Individual Counsel, and being at present in arrest by your order at this station, pending preferment and processing of charges against me, herein and hereby request to be represented by counsel as follows and I do further request that the within named counsel be granted permission to see me, without further delay, for purpose of adequately preparing my defense.

Military Counsel: 1st Lt. Edward K. Nichols Jr. 0-5566518

Regional Hospital, Fort Knox, Kentucky

Civilian Counsel: William H. Hastie, Esq.

Howard University Law School Washington, D.C.

And I do further fully understand that I must of necessity provide all expenses incident to the retention of counsel as designated hereinbefore.

James C. Warren

Flight Officer, A.C.

The Baumgardner Affair

Col. Selway's problems with the 104 black officers was not his only major problem. He had another pressing matter suddenly thrust upon him.

The Base Provost Marshal's position is comparable to the chief of police of a city. He is the top lawman in the Group. Maj. G. F. Baumgardner was the Base Provost Marshal for the 477th. Baumgardner should never have been allowed in the Army to begin with, and he certainly should not have been a commissioned officer. In addition, he had had no training in any of the administrative duties as a Provost Marshal. That he was assigned to a base, and to a high-caliber black organization, was incredible. He was involved in the policing of an organization of carefully selected men. This assignment had to be deliberate.

Lt. Col. E. E. Schaefer, from the Inspector General's office, made an inspection of the Provost Marshal activities at Freeman Field and submitted a report to Hunter. As a result of this report, on April 20, 1945, Hunter wrote a scathing letter to Selway. Hunter was very specific: "The large number of discrepancies noted and the operational inefficiency disclosed by this report indicate to me that there has been gross negligence and dereliction of duty by those charged with the proper performance of Provost Marshal's functions. There is also every indication that you have not exercised the necessary supervision and administrative control of Provost Marshal and security matters, thus allowing the unsatisfactory condition outlined in this report to develop and continue."

It is important to keep in mind that this Provost Marshal was supervising the arrest of black officers, and posting guards at the Officers Club Number Two to prevent qualified officers from using the club. Lt. Rogers was under orders from this Provost Marshal on the night of April 5, 1945.

Hunter's continued recommendations were equally clear:

"It is my desire that you take immediate action of a corrective nature to ensure the following:

"a. That Maj, G.F. Baumgardner be relieved of all Provost Marshal duties, that he receive an efficiency rating in keeping with the unsatisfactory performance of his duties while Provost Marshal, and that reclassification proceedings be initiated.

"b. That 2nd Lts. James M. Rice and Robert O. Harrison be relieved from the guard section of the 387th Air Service Group and replaced with competent officers."

The two officers mentioned above had been in attendance at the club on the night of April 5, 1945. They later made statements in support of Lt. Rogers immediately after the arrest of the first group of officers.

Selway had received these instructions by telephone earlier. In his reply to Gen. Hunter on April 25, 1945, he stated that he had relieved Maj. Baumgardner on April 11, 1945. However, in this letter to Hunter, Selway offered support for Baumgardner. In his letter of April 25, 1945, Selway stated that "during the tense period, Maj. Baumgardner did spend all his time on the post." He further defended him by pointing out that "it was his understanding that Maj. Baumgardner was sent to this program as an experienced and strong Provost Marshal."[43]

Investigation disclosed that in civilian life Baumgardner was a plain-clothes detective for the city police force of Dayton, Ohio—he was under two suspended indictments in that city for killing two Negroes. He had not had training in any of the administrative duties as a Provost Marshal.

One paragraph of Selway's reply to Hunter ranks as one of the most preposterous statements made at any time during this whole incident. Worse, it is a cruel insult to the black officers of this command. Selway stated, "With further reference to Paragraph 4a, it is felt that Maj. G. F. Baumgardner, in view of his good record in the Army, including two-and-a-quarter years overseas in CBI Theater, and in view of the fact that he was entirely unfamiliar with the duties and requirements of the Provost Marshal, and he acted as such for a limited time (five weeks at this Base), should be considered as malassigned in this position, rather than incompetent. It is requested that reconsideration be given to the desire that Maj. Baumgardner be reclassified."[44]

Selway's recommendation is unbelievable. He is not only disregarding the recorded evidence of his poor performance as a Provost Marshal of the 477th Bombardment Group, but is totally ignoring Baumgardner's obvious hatred of blacks, as evidenced by his record of murder of blacks in civilian life. In retrospect, it seems odd that there is no evidence that Baumgardner's performance, and his relief of duty, was discussed over the telephone. Could this subject have been too hot to handle over the telephone?

Formation of North American B-25s. F/O Warren is the Lead Navigator.

B-25 crew at
Godman Field.

Twin-Engine Pilot Class at Tuskegee.

Crew Chief checking his aircraft on Godman Field flight line.

F/O Warren in front of his aircraft.

F/O Warren and Lt. Harold Hillery leaving Godman for Louisville.

F/O Warren in the cockpit of a B-25 at Godman Field.

Briefing session at Godman Field. Briefing Officer 1st Lt. Perry Hudson. Seated l-r: F/O Toler, Capt. Jamison, 1st Lt. Ellis, 1st Lt. Briggs, Capt. Ellsbury. Standing l-r: 1st Lt. Bynum, 1st Lt. Blue, 1st Lt. Groves.

Capt. Stanton, 1st. Lt. Ellis, F/O Warren, and 2nd Lt. Roberts leave Godman Field for some recreation.

Maj. Gen. Frank O.D. (Monk) Hunter, with his ever-present swagger stick, and Col. Robert Selway. *U.S.A.F. photograph, Office of Air Force History.*

Col. Benjamin O. Davis, Jr., Commander,
477th Composite Group at Godman Field.

61 PILOTS ARRESTED

Offense?—Visiting White Officers' Club

477th Bomber Squadron Involved

By CHARLIE DAVIS, Indianapolis Bureau

FREEMAN FIELD, SEYMOUR, Ind.—Training of Negro officers at this air base was halted Thursday when sixty-one members of the replacement group of the 477th Bombardment Group were confined to quarters. The order was issued by Col. Robert Selway, commander of the group, and arose when the men entered the officers club on the post set aside for white personnel, and were asked to leave.

The men refused and MP's were called to place them under arrest. As they fled from the palatial club, their names were taken and the next day they were confined.

Due to a story appearing in The Courier last week, news reporters and correspondents are excluded from the strike gate and a grim vigilance was kept at the gate during Easter.

THE PITTSBURGH COURIER

NATIONAL EDITION

10c PER COPY

These 477th Bombardment Officers Bombard Jim Crow

...ME OF THE ONE-HUNDRED-AND-ONE officers recently arrested ...Freeman Field, Ind., because they attempted to enter an officers' ...b from which Negroes had been barred. Here they are with their ...sonal belongings lined up on a ramp. As their names were called ...y were placed on a C-47 Transport Plane and carried to Godman ...d, Ky., for confinement. Photographers of the outfit—the 447th ...mbardment Group—were on the scene and snapped pictures—the ...ority of which were destroyed on the scene by order of Col. Selway.

However, the above and a few others were saved. The officers are first and second lieutenants and flight officers. In the background one can see a bus that was the only one used to bring the officers from the barracks to the plane—the others were trucks as you can see to the right of the photo. Meanwhile it is reported, but not officially confirmed, that Col. Selway's command at Godman and Freeman fields will be lifted—pending conclusion of an investigation.

Headline and photograph from the *Pittsburgh Courier*.

9

Back at Freeman Field

Col. Selway, with his riding crop firmly in place and ever-present Kleenex in hand, no doubt smiled as the six C-47s with the 101 arrested officers aboard lifted off the runway at Freeman Field, circled left, and headed in a southeastern direction toward Godman Field, Kentucky. Now he had the bad apples out of the barrel. Things would be calm, serene and peaceful at Freeman once again. How wrong he was! The remaining "apples in the barrel," the black officers still at Freeman, were determined to keep the pressure on until Officers Club Number Two was closed permanently, until Base Regulation 85-2 was rescinded, or until the clubs were administered in accordance with Army Regulation 210-10, Paragraph 19.

Later, on that evening of April 13, 1945, Selway issued orders that Officers Club Number Two be immediately closed. He had just received word that several cars with black officers had passed by the club. He called for his Deputy Commander, Lt. Col. Pattison, and Col. Harris, the visiting Inspector General from the Air Staff, to join him. The three conspirators hurried down to our BOQ area, disdaining the use of the Colonel's staff car. Instead, they used Selway's private automobile, hoping for an element of surprise. As Selway described the scene to Gen. Hunter, "They had two large groups formed up there in their blouses, standing there very sullen. I asked them if it was their intent to violate any regulations or to test any, and got no reply." Of course he got no reply to such a question. But the truth was that if that club had remained open, many of the black officers would have entered, and the authorities would have had to arrest another group.

How Lowell M. Trice Gets on the Field

Col. Selway had no clear idea of what the situation was at the moment that he was talking to the group. He would have been extremely upset and severely disturbed had he known that Lowell M. Trice was among the group he was addressing. Trice had called our press liaison person, Lt. Weldon "Bootie" Green, and indicated that he wanted to come out and apprise the situation now that the arrested group had been transported away. How Trice infiltrated the field is an interesting story. 1st. Lt. William "Bill" Ellis tells it this way:

"Lt. Herman 'Rocky' Campbell, who owned a car, Bootie Green, and I went in to Indianapolis and picked up Mr. Trice. Trice was somewhat disabled, and walked with the aid of a crutch. As we approached the guard gate entrance to Freeman Field, we had to put Trice and his crutch on the floor of the car and spread a blanket over him, while Bootie sat in the back seat, shielding him from sight. We saluted and drove through the gate without a hitch. He was in the audience when Colonel Selway and his group came down to the area. In fact, someone noticed that Trice had on his porkpie hat and thick glasses. They surrounded him, and removed his hat and glasses so that he wouldn't be so readily identifiable as a non-military person.

"Selway, in his own way, attempted to talk to the group. He said, 'I want to talk to your spokesman, and we can straighten this out.' Lt. Col. Pattison got out and came around in front of the car. He looked directly at Bill Ellis and asked, 'Where is your spokesman? Are you Bill, the spokesman?' Of course Bill said, 'No, Sir.' Joe Whitten, who was back in the crowd where he could not be easily identified, spoke up and said, 'Sir, we have no spokesman.'"[45]

Trice listened to what was going on between Selway and the black officers, and talked to the officers after Selway had left. He now had experienced the situation at first hand, and he had gained a great amount of information from the officers remaining at Freeman Field. When he returned to Indianapolis and the *Indianapolis Recorder,* he had quite a lot to write about, and write he did.

Selway returned to his office and immediately called Hunter to make a report on the encounter. Hunter eagerly wondered if he could get some additional charges on the officers.

"Why didn't you order them back to their quarters?" asked Hunter.

"They broke up and we were talking to them in a group. They hadn't done anything wrong," replied Selway.

"Were they insolent? Insubordinate?" asked Hunter hopefully.

Hunter simply would not give up. He was hopeful that we would be foolish enough to commit some stupid act so he could lash out with all his authority and court-martial many more of the officers. We were too disciplined to act in such a manner that he could bring additional charges of insolence or insubordination.

"No, Sir, they were very polite," replied Selway.

"Did you order them to disband and go back to their quarters?" continued Hunter.

"They were breaking up and were headed back, and they hadn't done anything wrong, so I didn't want to say any word they could get me on as they hadn't done anything wrong."

"That's all right, but you're the Commander," insisted Hunter.

"Yes, Sir. There were a lot of white officers, and their wives and babies and everything in the Club, and I'm sure there would have been some jostling, and the white officers are pretty fed up with them, and I'm afraid they would have swung on them and we would have had a riot on our hands. The whites are plenty mad at them, so I'm glad we did not have any riot. I'd hate to present the new administration with something."

"Well, I still wouldn't have closed the Club. I would have had the women and children out of the Club, but I would have let them come. And then you would have brought the thing to a head."

"And they wanted a mass incident, too; that's what he said," Selway said, referring to his "spy." His spies were doing a sorry job. In certain situations, it would be most beneficial to have someone giving the enemy false information and getting some information in return, but in this situation we would have preferred that no one attempt to act as a "mole" in the enemy camp. Our hope was that Hunter and staff would reveal their diabolic plan for the destruction of the 477th in such a crude or blatant way that the War Department would be forced by public pressure to remove them from the command of the 477th. Our goal was to complete our training and get to combat, and prove that we could perform effectively as a medium bomb group.

"I think it would have been fine if they had a mass incident, if they want to have it. It would have clarified the air," said Hunter. Hunter wanted Selway to keep the Club open, and only keep the women and children out. He wanted a confrontation. He saw this as one way he could justify the way he was handling the Group. Selway did not relish such a confrontation, and finally persuaded Hunter to allow him to keep the Club closed.[46]

Hunter had forbidden Selway and others of his staff to refer to Officers Club Number Two as "the white Officers Club." Throughout this incident, he had insisted that the Club was simply a club reserved for instructor and supervisor personnel, that it was not a black or white club. However, in his rush to relay the latest news to Gen. Owens, Hunter used the "magic phrase."

"Listen," began Hunter, "From your Air Inspector's office, Colonel Harris is out at Freeman. And last night Selway called me up, he got word from one of the colored officers, who tells him things from time to time that they were forming over in the colored area and they were going to come over, all of them, and bust into the white Officers Club. Selway was afraid that the attitude of the minority of white officers is such that if somebody pushes them, they're going to start something. So, he closed his club. I recommend and request that a battalion of Military Police be sent out to that place. We either have got to give way to them, or we've got to enforce discipline. Now, I'd do the same thing with the whites. I'm not recognizing color one way or the other."

Hunter, however, was concerned that angry blacks might get touched off. There were some 400 black officers, in addition to the enlisted men, which made a minority of the whites at Freeman. His other concern was that the whites were getting antagonistic, which he considered perfectly natural. He saw this as a setting for violence, which he feared.

"Now if we..." began Owens, but he was again interrupted by Hunter.

"I recommend that over taking them back to Godman," continued Hunter. "Godman cannot handle them... the whole business... there's no room, but if we take them back there, that's giving way. And they talk about sending them to war. If they can't be handled at Freeman Field, how are they going to be handled when they go to war?" Here Hunter admitted that Godman was inadequate.

"That's right," agreed Owens.

"I recommend we keep them right there, and put enough white MPs in there so we give them orders and, if necessary, if they all mass, why, we can handle them en masse." Again Hunter was talking out of the other side of his mouth.

"I'll take this up with Barney just as soon as I can get in touch with him, Monk, and I'll call you back," replied Owens. Again he had fallen back on his now familiar answer, "I'll take it up with Barney."

"Thanks very much."

Owens later explained to Hunter the rejection of his request for a battalion of MPs. "General Giles and Lovett both decided against assigning a Military Police battalion there, but you have it on record that you've asked for it."

"I knew they would." Then Hunter got angry. "If they have any rioting, I'll go out there and clean it up myself, but I'm not going to start until they start rioting. They don't bluff me a bit, if they want to fight, I'd be glad to come out and join them." *He was really coming apart.*

"General Giles says let's not refer the charges to trial until we get the go-ahead from here," instructed Owens.[47]

Late in the afternoon of April 14, 1945, Hunter called Selway with more instructions: "Now, I want you to keep this under your hat, but, for planning purposes, make up your plans to move the 477th Group complete and the entire CCTS students' squadron to Godman Field. Now, that will leave the service group at Freeman, and you'll have to leave enough complement to handle that as a satellite field. When this happens, Godman will be the parent field again, and Freeman will be satellite to Godman. Now, you will most likely get orders to this effect in the next several days... but I wouldn't let this get out... but I'd make plans."

This recommended move came after the request for the battalion of Military Police had been denied. Hunter knew and had stated that Godman Field was an inadequate base for this bomb group. His recommendation was further clear evidence that the completion of combat training of this group was not his or the Army Air Forces' first priority.

Hunter had a few days to stew. As time went on, he became more jittery because deep in his heart he knew he was on very thin ice. He finally decided to confront Headquarters Air Force. After several rings, he got Gen. L. H. Hedrick, the Air Judge Advocate. "Some time ago I called up down there, I've forgotten whom I talked to, but I talked to somebody in the front office. I tried to talk to General Giles, but he wasn't there. I wanted to find out from the Air Inspector and you whether there was anything against having an officers club for trainees—and restricted to trainees—and another officers club for permanent party. They called me back and said it had been taken up with you and there was nothing against that, and it was done at many Air Force stations."

"I think Proctor called you," replied Hedrick.

"He took it up with your office," Hunter reminded him.

"I think, Hunter, that that's correct. The whole matter is in Personnel."

"No, that's the colored matter," said Hunter, hopefully.

"No, this is on the interpretation of Paragraph 19 of AR 210-10."

"Yes, but have you gotten *Command of Negro Troops,* a little War Department publication?" inquired Hunter.

"Well, it just involves the proposition of whether you can have separate club facilities."

"Well, have you read *Command of Negro Troops,* War Department Pamphlet Number 20-6? It goes through a great preamble and then it says: 'White soldiers by a majority favor racial separation in the Army. This holds true for both northerners and southerners. However sound their reasons may or may not be, this mass sentiment cannot be ignored.' Goes on down and says: 'War Department instructions advise that post exchanges, theaters, or sections of theaters, and other recreational facilities may be designated for the use of particular military units, not for the use of race or color. The burden of deciding whether or not there shall be some separation in the use of camp facilities is placed on the local command. The assumption of local conditions will be taken into account.'"

Hunter and other racist commanders had attempted to base their segregated policies on their interpretation of a War Department Pamphlet 20-6. A Pamphlet has much less administrative power than an Army Regulation. Using a Pamphlet to supersede a Regulation is contrary to the rules of army administration. These senior officers at FAF and HQ AAF were aware of this transgression of precedence; yet, to gain their goal, they took such a course of action anyway. What Hunter did not know was that the War Department had placed the entire controversy over this pamphlet in the hands of the McCloy Committee.

Hunter was hot under the collar as he continued his conversation with Gen. Hendrick. "What I want I get on the telephone, but unless I get it in writing, evidently I'm left holding the bag. I called up down there three or four weeks ago to ask whether you could have separate clubs for trainees, if I didn't mention colored, and they said they'd find out. They took it up with the Air Inspector, and said that they had gotten an opinion from the Air Inspector and the Judge Advocate of the Air Forces that it was O.K. Now, I haven't got that in writing, but I was told that."

Hunter was, after the fact, trying to get clarification of orders on which he had based his actions. Had he done this before he took such actions, the confrontation would have not gone that far. The commanders and instructors could have focused on the combat training, and the Group would have been well on the way to being combat ready.

Hunter Wants Something in Writing

"The only thing is, it leaves me out on the limb. I carry out instructions from Army Air Forces, then I try to get it in writing, and I can't," complained Hunter.

Throughout this incident there was no evidence that anyone pushed Hunter out on a limb. Hunter got himself out on that limb. It was almost as though Hunter was determined to get out there ever since the black fliers came under his command.

"Well, I'll tell you what you're getting from us in writing. They sent these three cases down to me the other day. Well, we're indicating in our comments that probably their defense will be set up on paragraph 19, and giving our views at least as to why we don't think it's a good defense, that we think you're right in doing what you did do. So we're certain…"

Hunter interrupted again, "I'm quite sure I'm doing what I'm supposed to do, but I got orders from a three-star general in the Army Air Forces on what I'm doing, but I also tried to get it in writing. They called me back and said it had been taken up, and it was in line with policies of the Army Air Forces to set up trainee clubs where they could for the trainees, and permanent party clubs for the permanent party and keep them separate. Proctor was the man, I'd forgotten even his name, but he told me it had been taken up with the Air Inspector and the Judge Advocate General, and that was the opinion of both.

"He didn't talk with me, but he talked, I think, probably with somebody in my office, so it's the same thing."

Hunter was not satisfied with this. He knew that his "irons were in the fire." He had gone a long way. Now that the public had found out about it, he had put the Army Air Forces in an embarrassing position. The Air Force was not very happy, to say the least.

"You see, what I'm after is not a future ruling. I'm after a ruling to substantiate what I have done."

"So far as my opinion goes, you've got it right now, man. I think you're absolutely correct, and I think that you were told it was correct," soothed Hedrick.

Hunter was close to panic. He wanted someone in higher headquarters to do something that he should have known they would not do.

"I'm writing a letter on the whole subject to Army Air Forces right now, and I'm putting my cards on the table. I've tried to do this thing, handle it just smoothly and all that, but now I've got an impossible situation where I've got a colored group about to go to war, and I'm in an impossible situation out there right now. They refuse to comply with orders. It's mass sedition, and I'm putting it right down on paper, and they won't give me the military authority to handle it, and it puts me in a very bad position, and it means in the future I can't handle them at all. They told me when I moved out of Selfridge... before I was allowed to move... Army Air Forces told me to have dual clubs at Walterboro and Godman before I could move. They held up the movement until I had them."

There were never two clubs at Godman. What Selway had was a snooze arrangement with the Fort Knox Officers Club so that your white officers could be members or guests, but not black officers.

"Yes, so I think that's what's coming out because the Service Forces—and, I understand, the Ground Forces—are in accord on just the same recommendation that we want to make, and I'm pretty sure that's what's going to come out of the War Department."

"Yes, bus in the meantime, I've got a unit that has shown collective disregard for constituted authority, and have gotten by with it. And I don't like it."

"Well, I don't blame you. Personnel here has got this paper and they're carrying the ball. They haven't sent it down to me, on making the recommendations."

I know what they're going to do, and I've recommended against it—you've given me all the dope I want. Thanks very much," replied an upset Hunter.

"O.K.," replied Hedrick, ending the conversation.[48]

You're right, General. You were in the position that we expected you to be when we started the protest. You could have been a hero. History would have recorded your command of this black bomber group in the glowing terms reserved for military heroes if you had taken this great opportunity that you were given and accepted this demanding leadership role with class, and viewed that command as an opportunity to take a giant step forward, and not as a noble experiment which you were to insist on destroying. What a difference it would have made in this country's history, and in your image, had you accepted this position, this command, and treated the black fliers as human beings. That group, those outstanding young men were willing to give their lives for their country in this glorious fight for democracy. Had you properly accepted this challenge, you would have given them one of your finest commanders to lead them. You would have selected instructors who valued these men for the content of their character and minds, and not by the color of their skin. Gen. Hunter, there were many such men available in the Army Air Forces from which to select just such a commander. You should have welcomed these young patriots to Selfridge Field and made them feel that their sacrifice would not be in vain. You should have ensured that their fledgling skills as fighter pilots would be nurtured with the greatest of care.

The men who lost their lives at Selfridge, were they given a fair chance? It was reported in an unsigned letter from a lieutenant assigned to the 332nd Fighter Group at Selfridge, to the Philadelphia Tribune, *October 2, 1943, that "they were forced to fly in every type of weather*[49] *and had lost Lts. Nathaniel Hill and Linson Blackney that way." Is their blood on your hands? Lts. Nathaniel Hill, Charles Dickerson, Jerome Edwards, Vincent J. Mason, my very good friend: Cornelius "Butch" May, my classmate: Frank H. Moody, Leon Purchase, Sidat Singh, Nathaniel Rayburg, Paul C. Simmons, William Walker, and Johnson C. Wells. All lost their lives at Selfridge. If you would have given more attention to their training than to what Officers Clubs they would use, would this have saved one life? Gen. Hunter, we, the Tuskegee Airmen, hold you responsible for the lives of these men.*

It was surprising that these high officials were not as aware of the thinking in the Services Forces and the Ground Forces as they thought they were. Had all the individuals involved been more informed, I feel that the changes that we wanted would have been effected sooner. The activities of the McCloy Committee illustrate a different viewpoint.

The War Department asked the McCloy Advisory Committee on Special Troop Policies to make recommendations on changes to War Department Pamphlet 20-6. The McCloy Committee made certain recommendations and sent these proposed changes to the different services for their recommendations. As predicted by Col. Hedrick, the Army Air Forces opposed the suggested changes, and suggested that the last paragraph on page 14 of the pamphlet be rewritten as follows:

"As a practical matter regulation of this problem must be handled in coordination with accepted social customs. For the War Department to attempt the solution by regulation of a complicated social problem which has perplexed this country for a number of years is bound to produce diversions that may go so far as to affect the full effectiveness of our war effort. The intermingling of the races in messing and housing would not only be a variation from well established policies of the Department, but it does not accord with the existing customs of the country as a whole."

The Army Air Forces insisted further: "The proposed amendment to War Department Pamphlet 20-6, which will make officers clubs available without discrimination to both white and colored officers, is not considered to be in the best interest of the service. It is believed that the provision of separate, comparable, but not reciprocal facilities, as recommended by the Commanding General, Army Air Forces, 21 April 1945, in Disposition Form to Army Service Forces, subject: 'Alleged Segregation of Negro and White Officers Clubs at Fort Huachuca, Arizona,' offers the only reasonable solution."[50]

The Army Air Forces justify this belief further: "Officers clubs are social centers that supplement the home of the members. They offer a social outlet with greater scope of contact and activity than possible in the confines of a home. The officer's entire family participates in club activities. Thus far, in the history of this country, it has not been the custom for whites and Negroes to intermingle socially either in homes or clubs. It is believed the Army should follow the usages and customs of the country as a whole rather than attempt to depart from accepted practices and establish social customs which are at variance with those existing in the country as a whole. The desires and interests of the white element in the Army in regard to the intermingling of whites and negroes in the officers clubs are as deserving of consideration as those of the negroes. These desires should be respected and, so long as the negro officers have comparable club facilities, it is strongly urged that there is no abuse of their rights as officers or citizens."

The Army Air Forces reply was written and signed by Brigadier Gen. Ray L. Owens, Deputy Chief of the Air Staff.[51] (*Use of lower case "n" in Negro is noted in the report.*)

It must be noted that the Army Services Forces' suggested change to the last paragraph on page 14 was positive, and in favor of non-discrimination.

Maj. Gen. Joe N. Dalton wrote: "War Department instructions provide that post exchanges and theaters, or sections of theaters, and other recreational facilities may be designated for the use of particular military units, but not for the use of a certain race or color group. The burden of deciding whether or not there shall be some separation in the use of camp facilities is placed on the local command. Existing instructions make it clear that it is the policy of the War Department to provide equal facilities for off-duty activities to all personnel without discrimination."[52]

The Organization and Training Division of the War Department General Staff also supported the non-separation policy. Maj. Gen. Edwards wrote: "I do not believe the proposed change in War Department Pamphlet 20-6 is as clear-cut as it should be. I suggest the following:

"'Where conditions make it desirable, War Department instructions permit the local commander to provide separate recreational facilities, such as post exchanges, theaters or sections of theaters, for the use of particular military units. However, it is the basic policy of the War Department that the provision of such separate facility does not permit the exclusion, on the basis of race or color, of any member of the military service from using any and all such facilities established in public buildings. Army Regulation 210-10, Paragraph 19, is explicit in defining the application of this policy to membership in officers clubs, messes, or similar social organizations.'"[53]

Hunter Continues to Seek Approval

At every turn now Gen. Hunter is trying to get firm approval of his actions from command levels higher up. He is not as inept as he seems to be at times. He simply is not swift enough. The train seems to have just left each time he decides to take a ride.

Hunter, not having found a satisfactory solution for his problem, made a foolhardy move. He wrote to Gen. "Hap" Arnold, asking for guidance should he be confronted with another such incident. He was asking for, and hoping to receive, approval from the Chief of the Air Forces to segregate and discriminate as he wished in his command. Arnold did not want the group, and he agreed with Hunter's beliefs, but he was determined not to become identified with any action that supported Hunter and a recommendation of dissolution. It was too hot, politically.

Each staff member hoped that a decision would be made by someone else, which would do the job for them, and they could all go home happy. The 477th Bombardment Group was a growing thorn in the side of the white Army Air Forces.

All the staff at Headquarters Air Forces wanted the 477th to go away, especially when talking to each other. One staff member would recommend an action and it would be approved. Then, someone else would make another recommendation and it would also be approved, but no one wanted to be held responsible for actually recommending and approving dissolution of the 477th.

Gen. Ray L. Owens, the Chief of Staff of Headquarters Air Forces, and Gen. Arnold's chief administrator, called Hunter to tell him, in so many words, that the Chief was not asleep at the switch, and knew what he was trying to do, but Arnold would not give him anything in writing. Hunter was not in, and Owens began the following conversation with Gen. Glenn: "I wanted to call General Hunter and tell him that with reference to this letter that he wrote down to the Chief of the Air Forces some time ago asking for guidance in case another incident was to come up."

"Yes, I know the one," answered Glenn.

"Well, naturally that's a little hard for the Chief to answer that one, except he said to tell General Hunter that we are perfectly pleased and happy, and satisfied with the action he took in the last case. This thing has been investigated by the Inspector General, and it has gone through Personnel, who has approved the Inspector General's investigation, and has gone through the Chief of Staff up to the McCloy Board." *This reply by Owens did not catch anyone by surprise. Could this little game have continued this long without the Chief of Staff, Gen. Arnold's approval?*

"The what?" inquired Glenn.

Had this business not been so serious this conversation would have seemed most hilarious. The Chief of Staff of a numbered Air Force did not know of the existence of an Assistant Under Secretary of War, nor did he know anything about the committee that he headed. What follows is a real indication of the low level of awareness of these people about the race problem. Also, they were not aware of the proposed changes being considered by the McCloy Board.

Owens explained: "The McCloy Board. He is the Assistant Under Secretary of War. He has a board that is supposed to handle all colored affairs."

"Is he colored?" a puzzled Glenn asked.

"No, he's not, though he has one on his staff. Just as soon as the McCloy Board acts on this, the Commanding General, Army Air Forces, will be able to answer General Hunter with a definite reply, but just in the event anything should happen before this reply is given us, the Chief here feels that his action in the past was perfectly all right, it was legitimate. He is satisfied with it, and if another event were to come up, he hopes he will handle it in the same manner.

"I asked Bill Welsh this morning at 8:30 if they had made their decision yet on what to do, and he said, of course, that was what they would like to do, and we all agree with that, but they hadn't come to a full decision yet. If they have today, they have taken it up with Ira and had it approved there, I don't know. That's contrary to what General Marshall had agreed to with Giles," Owens said.

"That's exactly the point. General Giles made that recommendation, and it was my understanding General Marshall approved it and now they are not doing that at all, which is, after all, a solution of a temporary expedient, but it's going to cause future trouble. It isn't going to remedy the trouble that could be rectified if this other action were taken which has already been approved by General Marshall. I can't understand that," replied a confused Glenn.

"I don't believe that. I really don't, because I asked Bill Welsh this morning at 8:30. I said there is a board, I had appointed a board at the direction of the Chief, consisting of Welsh, Herman, and Wilson, to figure out plans to implement this inactivating and demobilization of the 477th and associate units, in compliance with General Marshall's approved recommendation to Giles. And he said, 'Well, the Board hasn't gotten together on that.' That was at 8:30 this morning, but he said, 'We are going to.'"

"At 11:30, Bill Streett called me and said, 'Here is the latest that I have just gotten from Welsh,'" stated Glenn.

"I will have to find out about that."

"It's to send two squadrons over shortly, and it keeps the problem in our lap because we will have to be training replacement crews for them right along and send them out to a theater where they are going to come back with a lot of ribbons all over them. Whether they do anything or not for the good of the country, it is going to make things even worse eventually," lamented Glenn.

"Sure it is. When they come back they will be cockier than ever and harder to control."

"That's exactly it."

"The way to control them is to knock them off now while we can."

"They got a marvelous opportunity you know."

"Personnel has made some recommendations which have been approved by this McCloy Board that will put them in their places, and that was in compliance with the Inspector General's recommendations. I am telling you this as a little inside dope that I have that the Inspector General was without any criticism whatsoever of General Hunter or the Commanding Officer out at Freeman Field. The fact is he commended their action."

"I gave General Hunter that message I had from Bill Streett, and he hit the ceiling."

"I hope the McCloy Board will settle this thing, and Personnel is immediately ready to publish a revision of that Paragraph 19 of AR 210-10 that these people base their stand on. If they do that within the next two or three days, then the Chief of Air Corps can go ahead and answer Monk's letter, and give him a direct answer on the question that he asked." said Owens.

"I will tell General Hunter…" agreed Glenn.

"Get hold of Welsh and find out what this other story is," instructed Owens.

"I wish you would read that last endorsement of that last letter that Monk sent down."

"It's in my office."[54]

The McCloy Board did not make the recommendations that they had hoped. The Board recommended just the opposite:

"The report submitted by the Army Air Forces suggests, in substance, that the Army return to a policy of separate and equal facilities for white and Negro personnel. Such a policy, in the Boards' opinion, would be a step backward and would reverse the position taken by the War Department in the Selfridge Field case in which the same issues were involved."[55]

10

"The Smoking Gun"

The preoccupation of Gen. Hunter and Col. Selway with keeping blacks in their place had obscured the single most important obligation of command: the preparation of the 477th Bombardment Group for entering the combat zone and participating in the battle against the enemy.

Hunter was not merely actively antagonistic to the Group's becoming combat ready, he had decided that the 477th could never be ready for overseas deployment. Blacks could not be expected to perform satisfactorily enough for combat ready status.

Gen. Giles had not overlooked this aspect of the situation during his inspection trip to Freeman Field, and, upon his return to Washington, he discussed the status with Gen. Welsh. Welsh's response was to look at the record, and what he saw was not very encouraging. There was good reason for his pessimism. For one year and eleven months, training had not been the real mission of the 477th, and everybody knew it. The prime purpose at Godman had been to keep the trainee personnel occupied in order that there would be no dissension on their part which would be brought to the attention of the public through the medium of the press. The ugly truth was that, under pressure of inspection, Hunter made just such an admission a month later: "Due to excessive time available, additional types of flight training had to be instituted for morale purposes."

Welsh's office had been trying to get a correct status on the 477th's readiness training for some time from First Air Forces Headquarters, and it had not received any consistent status reports.

Gen. Welsh called Col. Malcolm N. Stewart, the acting Chief of Training at Headquarters First Air Force, and began, "General Giles had commented that he thought the strength of the whites there could be reduced considerably, and that consideration had been given to replace all of the squadron officers with colored."

Col. Stewart was nervous at the prospect of discussing the training situation of the 477th because he knew that its present status was unjustifiable. He began, " I believe a letter was written advocating that thing, or requesting our judgment in the matter, and we approved of it as soon as white officers become available and demonstrate a proficiency for such duty."

"As soon as *colored* officers," Welsh corrected Stewart.

"I mean colored officers," Stewart hastily added, somewhat sheepishly.

"Why don't you put them in there; you've got to accept a degree of efficiency less than you would expect in the white CCTS."

"Oh, yes, we know that."

"And, if they are going to have colored organizations, they ought to do the best they can with what they have got, and, if they don't pay dividends, we shouldn't have them."

"We have believed that all along. They don't pay dividends, they are not going to pay dividends, and we are pretty well convinced they don't want to go to war, some of them. That is an injustice to some of them because some of them are honest and want to go to war," replied Stewart, sticking to the party line here, as well as trying to justify the current status the training.

"That's right, and, at any rate, we are on unfirm ground until we have at least given them a chance," pointed out Welsh.

"That's correct, and we have gone on record in answering your letter... I believe I signed it, if I am not mistaken, while I was acting Chief of Staff... that they would be replaced as soon as competent colored officers were developed or returned to us, capable of taking over the squadron jobs."

Stewart was correct in his understanding of the original plan for staffing. Bringing the black units on line began with the 332nd at Selfridge, which saw Col. Benjamin O. Davis Jr., taking command and taking the group overseas. However, this procedure deteriorated almost immediately in the 477th. Instead of advancing deserving black officers to command positions, this unit became little more than a promotion mill for white officers of the FAF. When a white officer was assigned to a staff position, he was almost immediately promoted to the rank required by that position. After a minimum tenure in the position, he moved on, and another would be assigned.

Gen. Welsh changed the subject, and began to discuss the original reason for his call. "I hate to bother you all so much on this, but it is something that pops close to the throne here, and if you don't have the information, you can't provide an answer, and you might provide the wrong answer in the necessity of giving one. Some of the things I can't understand exactly is the flying time of some of those individuals. There are pilots that are listed with 150 hours twin-engine time, B-25 time as co-pilots. Any pilot that has had 150 hours co-pilot should be a first pilot."

"That's quite right," admitted Stewart.

"Now I know that everybody will come back and say that you're afraid to turn them loose.' "

Stewart interrupted defensively, "No, that isn't the idea, necessarily. We are not afraid to turn them loose. Some of those co-pilots are just as good as the first pilots. The thing there is that we have not had enough airplanes to make up complete crews. Therefore, we have been obliged to make them fly in the airplanes we have, and the ones that are getting all the time as co-pilots are naturally the ones that are junior to the first pilots."

"But they are all checked off?" questioned Welsh.

"They are all checked off and available as first pilots, but we just haven't had the airplanes to make up the crews, and we have not had the gunners and the rest of the crew— particularly navigators and bombardiers that are qualified to make up the full crews. Therefore, we have been unable to even start the training."

Welsh continued to press Stewart. "From the information I get, you have 64 crews complete in the group."

"I wouldn't know just exactly how many, it's something like that," replied Stewart weakly.

Welsh impatiently asked, "I wonder if it wouldn't be a good idea to let me know exactly what you need in all respects."

"Yes, I think there is correspondence down there to that effect, but I will go back over it and send you copies of it."

"If it is down here, I will have McTague and someone working on it here to see if you are short anybody. The impression I got in the inventory here is that you are over instead of short," pressed Welsh.

"We are over in some categories, and very short in others. In other words, we don't have navigators. We don't have sufficient navigators to make full crews. We don't have sufficient trained bombardiers to make full crews." *Col. Stewart was scrambling now for answers, but he gave the wrong answer.*

"You mean graduate bombardiers?"

"That's right," added Stewart, hoping to get this one by Welsh.

"Thought we had too many, because we were screening them to put them back in the pilot program," replied Welsh, indicating that he was well informed and was not buying these excuses.

"No, I don't believe so; maybe I am in error on that, but I will tell you what I will do."

The fact is that six of the 13 officers, who were my classmates, were already dual-rated—qualified both as navigators and as bombardiers. More impressive yet, the six had been sent almost directly from bombardier school to Tuskegee Air Base for entry in pilot training, and four of them completed pilot training, becoming probably the first triple-rated officers in the Army Air Forces.

Welsh returned to the attack. "This inventory I have here you might check; it shows on March 13 in the CCTS there were seven pilots, 35 co-pilots, 65 navigators and bombardiers, 57 engineer-gunners, 59 radio-gunners, 62 armorers, and 24 rated officer-instructors, white, and two test flight engineers."

"That probably is about right." *Stewart was agreeing now as often as possible.*

"That would indicate a surplus of navigators and bombardiers."

"It looks that way, but remember we are doing two things; we are running a CCTS in conjunction with an OTU." *A very weak response by Stewart.*

"This showed that they had 64 complete crews. This group is equipped with 62 B-25-type aircraft, plus one Class 26. (*Class 26 indicates an aircraft in an unserviceable condition.*) At the present time has the following personnel: 'T/O (Table of Organization) strength, 64 crews. T/O plus reserve, 96 crews.' Then there is a footnote that says 25 crews short. So, that would indicate that there were 71 crews. I think that's a bit high."

"We are ordered to send 50 percent in addition to the OTU."

"I know that, but this said there is present the following personnel. I didn't think that you had 71 complete crews down there; I know that you had ***** (*cylinder changed and some of conversation not recorded*) 96."

"That's right, but I don't think we are going to make that… about 96, yes."

"Ninety-six is what you need?" asked Welsh.

"That's right, but I don't think we are going to make that. I think we are going to make about 91."

"What I want to know is how many you have. I can't get that from anybody," replied an exasperated Welsh.

"I will get that information and get it down to you."

"I have gotten this information from five different sources, and every one varies. I got it from Personnel, from Management and Control, from the records that were sent in from your office, and from calls direct to Godman, and all of them are in variance. So I would like to know just what the status of training of the 477th is. How many crews have they got that could go to war and when, and what do they need to make it ready to go to war, and what have they got in the CCTS?" Welsh asked.

From this question it is clear that at least one person at Headquarters Army Air Forces was interested in the combat

potential and the combat readiness training of the 477th
Bombardment Group.

"I can get that for you I am sure."

"That will help no end."

"I will get that, and I will try and show you some of the reasons for some of the things you asked me because I am quite sure that we have the answers here," said Stewart, hopefully.

"I'm sure you have, but we are in the position here that the further away you get from anything, the less you know about it."

"And sometimes that is a rather confusing situation down there in itself," said Stewart.

"That's right, so we are trying to help you out and will do everything we can to get this squared away, but there are questions coming up as to whether the 477th should go to war or not, or whether it *could* go to war."

"General Hunter doesn't think it's ready to go to war now."

Restating his belief that the Group could and should be sent to war, Gen. Welsh replied, "If it isn't, it never will be." *Gen. Welsh knew better than Hunter.*

"I don't think it ever will be, frankly," said Stewart, sticking to the party line all the way.

"So, I would say it's ready. I mean we have trained them, and there should be some spot in the Pacific where they could be put down there, in the Aleutians, or some other place."

"Yes, I suppose so, and yet, with all due respect to them, I believe that there are some of them that are honest and sincere in wanting to do the job right."

"Oh, unquestionably," replied Welsh.

"And yet, there are others that are bad eggs in a dozen, you know," Stewart replies, anxious to get away from discussing the training program.

"That's right; no question about it."

"And when you put one bad apple in a basketful, you are going to have a lot more unless you pull it out."

Welsh, still concerned about the training program, pressed Stewart again. "But the surprising thing here shows that in one report I got that the majority of those pilots are over 300 hours in B-25s, some of them up to 900 hours."

"That's right. They have been flying the pants off those airplanes that they had, but we have been unable to give them group training as a group because we just haven't had enough crews to make up a full crew," Stewart replied. *But again, he was wrong. We did have sufficient crews for training.*

"But you do have now with the 64 crews?" Welsh asked.

"I will have to check on that. I am not going to commit myself on that because I am not sure."

"I will appreciate your letting me know."

"Now, then, General Giles said in the relieving of Selway down there he wanted Monk to know that he didn't want anything put on his record, any adverse comment on his record. And I know Monk won't want to put an adverse comment on it."

"No, he is not given to doing things like that; he will put down what he thinks is a good fair estimate." *What Col. Stewart did not know is that Gen. Hunter had said in a previous telephone conversation the following: "He's going to get a very poor efficiency report out of me, although I know it's difficult thing, but I think he's handled it poorly."*

"That's right," said Welsh.

"Just a minute. General Giles concurs in that action doesn't he?"

"In relieving Selway?"

"Yes."

"Yes," said Welsh, replying more emphatically.

"All right. I think he has the jitters so bad that he is going to have a breakdown if we don't relieve him."

"I would get him out without delay," advised Welsh.

"That's right. We have somebody to go down there, and so I will tell the General about this."

"O.K., is there anything fresh coming up down there?"

"No, we haven't had an intelligence report in some time, but everything is quiet today."

"There doesn't seem to be any way out except to get them down to Knox."

"I don't know, I am a little leery of that because whenever you by any means indicate you are giving in to them, they just go that much stronger next time," said Stewart.

His reasoning was unclear, because we would not want to return to Godman Field, and would certainly not look at a move to Knox as a winning move that would have changed our attitudes.

"This regulation… this 210-10 that they base their plea on… is certainly all on their side."

"Sure, but 210-10 was also in existence at Fort Huachuca when the Army decided against them."

"Army never decided against them," replied Welsh, again indicating that he is more aware of the facts than is Stewart.

"Oh, yes, they approved the action taken at Huachuca in having separate ones designated by race," argued Stewart.

"They haven't yet. It is still up here now."

"I understood from the Judge Advocate that they had."

"No, it's up in Personnel now. I just called over about it, and they are trying to get the War Department to announce a policy and the War Department won't do it, other than that they announced in 210-10 and in that Air Force Letter 35-128, Recreational Facilities, on August 17, 1944."

"You know, there is a lot to be said on both sides. In other words, white people have got to have something to say, too."

"That's right," agreed Welsh.

"As a matter of fact, at Freeman we were trying to protect the minority. That sounds funny, but we were. There were 3000 against 300."

You're right, Colonel, it would have sounded funny, if it wasn't so tragic.

"I know that, and I have maintained all along that it's the whites that are being discriminated against in the Army, and not the colored," said Welsh.

"You can't beat them, you know. They're pretty smart. You know the old saying if you teach a hound dog a trick, you have to know more than the dog. That applies there, too."

"Our thought was that rather than create a condition… what I'm afraid of is this… if this thing gets out of hand, you may have some of the 'jig-a-boos' up there dropping in on you at Mitchell Field."

"Yes, we are probably going to have them anyhow."

"That's right. The suddenness of the President's death and everything this way, that if this is a forced issue right at this time, it's a foregone conclusion that an adverse decision will be given. If we can stave it off in some way for a period of time, and present a staff study based on the requirements for additional training, maybe we can eliminate the program gradually and accomplish our end."

By any standards, Gen. Welsh's unequivocal statement represented "the smoking gun." It was the clearest statement of the intent of the Air Staff that a member of the General Staff had made. It was very candid and to the point. The end objective was to eliminate the program.

No other interpretation of his comment is possible. One of the more deliberate actions that contributed to this end was the moving of the 477th, or elements of it, some 30 times since its formation. Keeping the group jumping from base to base throughout its career, mostly on bases that admittedly were the worst possible for black troops, as well as inadequate for the type of training that was needed, was a direct and measurable deterrent to training, third in importance perhaps only to the slow manning and to what are called "incidents."

The mismanagement of training, crew formation, record keeping, and scheduling of personnel to attend schools—all of these factors surely were deliberate. Of course, the authorities developed staff studies based on false conclusions and recommendations to support each of these delays. This is why a complete verbatim transcript of these telephone conversations is essential for understanding the statement.

"Maybe we can eliminate the program gradually and accomplish our end," is all the evidence anyone could require to understand why this 477th Bomb Group was not trained efficiently and made combat ready in the required amount of time.

Stewart was quick to agree with Gen. Welsh's candor. "Yes, I think also that, perhaps, waiting a little while will have a better effect on account of recent developments."

"So, all in all, we felt down here the best thing to do would be move back to Godman because there you could get by with the one club."

Again, the General put the plain truth out on the table. The command officers were willing to accept any restrictions on flying facilities simply to be able to control the use of the officers club on a base.

"That's right," agreed Stewart.

"I will get that to you just as quickly as we can get it together."[56]

The contents of this telephone conversation are unbelievable. The level of candidness expressed by the participants was certainly unusual. This conversation reveals disgusting, damaging, and precise information that applied to the whole program of the 477th Bombardment Group. A very interesting cat-and-mouse game was being played by Gen. Welsh with Col. Stewart. Welsh was getting information from Stewart that Stewart did not really want to reveal. Welsh was also letting Stewart know what a sorry job of training the First Air Force was doing. In his position as Chief of Staff of the Air Force for Training, this was quite a statement to make. Yet, Gen. Walsh revealed his own racist feelings. This conversation substantiates the conviction of some persons within the headquarters of AAF that the Group should be all black.

This conversation also reveals what we already knew, that the shortage of crew members was a lie. The truth was that there were sufficient crews available and that the pilots were, if anything, over-trained. More importantly, this Group should have completed its training and been transferred to an overseas theater on time.

Col. Stewart, in his position as the Training Officer for FAF, represented Gen. Hunter's view of training of this group. Therefore, his conversation is unmistakable evidence that Gen. Hunter's first priority was ensuring that there be no change in his segregation policies. His dominant interest was preventing any integration of officers clubs on bases under his command, and any mixing of the races in a social setting whatsoever. Correspondingly, the destruction of the 477th Bombardment Group remained a consistent objective.

11

Public Relations. The Dispute Over the Black Press

The black press was one of the most powerful tools that the blacks used in the fight for equal treatment in the Army Air Forces. The *Pittsburgh Courier* was by far the most widely circulated Negro newspaper in America, having expanded from a circulation of 126,962 in 1940 to more than 286,000 in 1947. In those years, its circulation was larger than the next two largest Negro newspapers combined. The *Courier* was considered so powerful that the War Department tried to bar its distribution, along with other Negro journals, from military posts. Henry L. Stimson, Secretary of War, John J. McCloy, Assistant Secretary of War for Negro Affairs, and others in the War Department blamed the Negro press for bad morale among black troops. Emanating out of the Justice Department were threats to try the Negro press for sedition. Some officials proposed to withhold newsprint allocations from all black newspapers.[57]

Were Negro newspapers in fact "agitators?" Was the Negro press to blame for racial tension and violence that accompanied the social upheaval of World War Two? Gen. Hunter certainly thought so. He constantly lambasted the Negro newspapers for fomenting race hatred by its alleged agitation of the Negro officers in the 477th and at other bases under his command. Often the battle raged heatedly.

It is noteworthy that the May 1945 issue of *Fortune* magazine undertook to do a frank, realistic survey of the Negro press, and appraised its character and contributions to

America. The study by newspaper analyst, James S. Twohey, would seem to have been a final, sweeping rebuttal to Hunter. Nevertheless, Hunter persisted in his venomous race-baiting comments, and continued to harp on the unfairness and the "agitator role" of the Negro newspapers.

This much-respected magazine of big business found in a study of the front pages of 28 Negro papers for one month that a total of 68 percent of all stories were devoted to Negro-white relations, in contrast with the 32 percent exclusively about Negroes. Breaking down the 68 percent, *Fortune* noted that 35 percent furthered friendly Negro-white relations. Eighteen percent were unfavorable to whites' conduct to Negroes, while 15 percent were neutral in attitude.

"Stories commenting favorably on Negro-white relations outweigh the protests by two to one," said *Fortune's* editors. "The stories of discrimination… are outnumbered by the stories of Negro-white co-operation." These findings were a direct contradiction to the breast-beating of Hunter, and those sometimes misinformed, sometimes slanderous whites who said that "the Negro press was too militant, too inflammatory." One newspaper, the *Chicago Defender,* noted that the *Fortune* article demonstrated with facts, and not fictional claims, about Negro newspapers, that essentially the Negro press was a positive force for unity and amity. "The Negro Press, on the other hand, stands on the untrammeled view that a positive approach to genuine Americanism means the granting of full, unfettered citizenship to the Negro. The Negro Press believes in complete equality for the darker brother. The Negro Press stresses a healthy and free relationship between the races. It publishes pictures and stories of mixed activity, because it feels that essentially the race problem resolves itself to white fear of the dark stranger.

When white Americans get to know, like, and respect Negroes as fellow humans, the race question will be ended.

"The Negro Press, for all the claims by rabid reactionaries that it overemphasizes protest, is accentuating the positive. *Fortune's* survey is the final proof of this salient, significant fact in racial relations."[58]

Gen. Hunter paid no attention to facts. Fortune's included, and demanded, absolute control of all press relations, especially any releases on the Freeman Field incident. Furthermore, he demanded and got even tighter control of Col. Selway in his relations with the press. He needed this control because he knew it would be easy for any reporter to discover what he was actually trying to do with the 477th.

Throughout this period, Hunter considered one reporter from a relatively small paper to be the greatest threat to his plans. The reporter was Lowell M. Trice, of the Indianapolis Recorder. *Each time Trice would show up at Freeman Field, Selway would find a way to get him off as fast as possible.*

Hunter expressed his concern about Trice with Selway in a telephone conversation on April 12, 1945, "Now, do you know whether that guy is still downtown there? In other words, I might put the FBI on him for fomenting disobedience and revolt in the Army."

Selway replied, "They tell me he was out there in that housing area last night. I sent out a message on the very first day when I caught him on the post, and I asked that action be taken through Washington to deny any of the personnel of that paper entrance on this federal reservation."

Hunter's phobia of the reporter and black newspapers was unrelenting. The information officers at Army Air Forces Headquarters were getting intense pressure from the War Department to respond to the press, and they attempted to relay that urgency to Hunter.

Hunter did not want any reporters to visit Freeman Field to interview Selway. He did not want Selway answering reporters unless Hunter had placed severe restrictions on what he could say. Most of all, Hunter was to be the only person to discuss this incident with the press people.

As a result of Hunter's stonewalling, the War Department again had to interfere in the management of the 477th program, this time in its relations with the press. On April 26, 1945, Col. Haddock, from the Bureau of Public Relations for the Air Force, called Hunter and read him the statement they wanted Selway to release about the incident.

This proposed statement was a retelling of the events using wording that attempted to make Hunter's policy and Selway's actions seem benign and proper and, further, to make it seem that these actions were completely in accord with existing War Department instructions.

The statement explained the offense as simply a number of trainee officers attempting to enter an exclusive club. They were not permitted to do so by the Assistant Provost Marshal, and three of the trainee officers had physically pushed him aside and entered the club. These three officers were now in arrest and awaiting court-martial. It reiterated the tale of the development of Base Regulation 85-2, and the refusal of 101 trainee officers to sign an endorsement that they had read and understood the regulation even after each had been given a lawful order by his commanding officer to do so. Their refusal was a violation of the 64th Article of War, which provides that any person subject to military law who willfully disobeys a lawful command by a superior officer shall suffer death or such other punishment as a court-martial may direct. As a result, 101 trainee officers were placed in arrest, and, on April 13, 1945, returned to Godman Field, where they were held in arrest in quarters.

Hunter was, as usual, hot under the collar when he realized he was no longer in command of the situation. He did not like to take orders. This had gotten him fired once before, but he persisted. He suggested changes in the press release. For example, he wanted Col. Haddock to avoid using the phrase, "pursuant to War Department orders." Hunter pointed out, "I didn't want to move them over there, I was ordered to."

Haddock rushed in and told Hunter to hold his fire. He wanted to read him another paragraph of the press release before he would listen to Hunter's argument. "General, let me read one more paragraph, and we'll go back to that, Sir:

"'On April 25, 1945, those 101 trainee officers were released from arrest in quarters, and have been given an administrative reprimand. Pursuant to War Department order, both clubs were closed and will remain closed while an investigation into the occurrences I have described is being completed by the War Department. Necessary measures to maintain good order and discipline will continue to be taken promptly as circumstances require.'"

Hunter, having had a moment to think about what was happening, replied, "The only objection I've got to it… it's almost verbatim with my statement… is that those clubs were closed by order of General Giles, and, also against my recommendation, those 101 were moved to Godman Field pursuant to his orders."

Hunter's statement, "It was against my recommendation those 101 were moved to Godman Field," was blatantly untrue. In his conversation with Gen. Kuter on April 12, 1945, Hunter said, "Selway's recommended, and I approved it, there will be 105 stewing around there in arrest in quarters. He wants to move them over to Godman, where they will prefer charges against them, and, pending your turning me loose to court-martial them, send them over to Godman to get the rotten apples out of that barrel so they won't stir up any more trouble." However, this type of action—of changing his statements to suit the moment—was typical of Hunter's actions throughout this incident.

Again, Hunter is bending the truth in every way and every time he can. Previously, when Gen. Kuter had asked Hunter how he would move the arrested officers to Godman, Hunter did not know. Hunter suggested by train or air, but complained that he did not have the air resources required. Later, Gen. Owens suggested the Troop Carrier Command. Kuter told Owens, "Call General Olds' headquarters and tell him to meet a request for air transportation for them from Freeman Field."

However, Haddock did not have the information contained in a the telephone conversation between Hunter and Kuter and Owens, so he had to rely only on Hunter's word. He added, "Fine, just one minute, Sir. ***** We'll put that in."

Hunter began to discuss the relations of Godman and Freeman Field as one being the satellite of the other. This detailed information confused Haddock. "Freeman was only a satellite because the bulk of the training was being done at Godman, and when they were transferred the reverse would be true, is that right?"

Hunter replied, "That's right. We took over from some other command, Freeman. Godman was the home station and Atterbury was the satellite. Then we got this beautiful, wonderful station that could accommodate the whole thing, so we closed out Atterbury, and moved the Group and the Service Group to Freeman from Godman, and later moved the CCTS personnel, and Freeman became the parent station and Godman a satellite." *This was getting complicated, but the reason soon becomes obvious.*

Haddock, a bit puzzled, said, "I see. It's a small point, as you say. It might be worth making here."

"I don't know—if you just leave out the 'satellite.' I don't know that you need to refer to that."

Then the plot began to come out. Haddock began to explain the cover-up scheme. "What we were doing is setting the stage for returning there, you see. Because questions might be legitimately asked, and this was anticipating. What we could say would be this, General: 'The First Air Force assumed control of Freeman Field March 1, 1945, moving the units involved from Godman Field, Kentucky, at which time there was placed into effect…' That just brings in Godman and identifies it. Then we can say, 'On April 13, they were returned to Godman Field'. We don't need to specify one or the other as a satellite."

"All right. Now, you aren't saying anything about the whole units being moved back now, are you?" asked Hunter.

"Not a thing, Sir."

"The papers have been after them on that. That's a secret order. Owens called me up yesterday, and I said that's a secret order, and I don't put out secret orders on movements during wartime."

"That's right."

"No, I have no objection, that statement is a correct statement."

"Fine, General, we'll make that change that you have suggested here."

Hunter never forgot that one of his dominant objectives was to get the War Department to place something in writing approving his activities. He saw this memo as a bit of approval as he asked, "Now, you aren't putting in there, and I'm perfectly willing to carry the load, the truth that they were released from arrest by orders from the War Department. If they want me to carry that for them, I don't mind," volunteered Hunter.

"Would you prefer to have it in there?" asked Haddock.

"I'd prefer it, yes, but I'm perfectly willing for it not to be in there. That is a fact."

"So that we might say, and it would be approved by you, 'On April 23, 1945, on orders of the War Department, these 101 trainee officers were released from arrest,'" replied Haddock.

"That is a correct statement. It is up to them if they want to put that in or not. Now, they don't care to say that this action has been with the approval of the War Department?"

"We don't know that, Sir. We haven't even taken it to them, sir."

"If they agree to that statement, I'd like the War Department to have nerve enough to say that the action taken has been with the full approval of the War Department," replied Hunter.

"Well, we'll put that in and see what happens."

"All right, fine."[59] *I can imagine Hunter smiling, thinking that he had at last got the War Department's approval in writing for his shenanigans.*

Selway Deals With the Press?

Meanwhile, back at Freeman Field, Selway was sweating out the pressure he was receiving from the press. He wanted to act as a commander should, and deal with the press on his own, but he knew better than to act without Hunter's approval. He did not have long to wait. Early on the morning of April 24, 1945, Hunter called. His first question was whether Selway had released the officers under arrest. Later,

Selway asked if "the public relations had called this morning?"

Hunter wasted no time in giving Selway further orders. "Here's the dope *(a favorite expression of his)*. You will make no statements. I'm expecting to have a press conference here tomorrow afternoon as soon as I get it cleared by the War Department, and to issue a statement. And I'm going to get into your hands a copy of that statement so you can release it out there. I do not want you to make any other statements, I do not want you to answer questions, and you can release the same statement that I'm releasing here. I'll read it to you on the phone and see if you agree with it: 'In handling the recent incidents at Freeman Field, I have refrained from recognizing any racial problems.' What comment have you got to make?"

Of course, Selway had none. "Perfect," he replied.

"Any inaccuracies in that statement?" asked Hunter.

Again Selway gave an enthusiastic response: "Absolutely correct." Hunter continued to instruct Selway: "All right. I want you to make no statements to this man from the *Sun (Chicago Sun-Times)* or anybody else until I send you a statement, and that's the one I want you to give the local people around there and anybody else."

Selway, still not realizing how tight the muzzle was, replied, "Yes, Sir. It will take about two or three hours because those birds always sit and cross-examine anyway."

Oh, no! That is not what Hunter wanted to happen.

"Don't let them. You can just give them this paper and that's all. I don't want you to be cross-examined and put in an embarrassing position. This is a full statement on the subject. You don't have to pass on the legality of the orders you get. I'm constituted authority to give you orders, and you're complying with my orders."[60]

The following day, Hunter called Selway back and told him that the press conference would be delayed further because the War Department was not going to allow him to make a statement. They had taken the public relations back in their hands completely. So, for now, Selway should refer anybody with questions about this incident to the War Department Bureau of Public Relations.

The War Department's reaction represented the degree of pressure that the nation, black citizens and politicians were exerting. This amount of concern at the highest level of command again indicated the importance of this incident. Press relations had been bungled from the beginning. One of the most serious public relations goofs occurred early on when the Military Police initially allowed a reporter from the *Chicago Sun-Times* on the base, and then the Public Relations Officer, Capt. Robert W. McIntosh, had him thrown off. This reporter was from a big-city daily newspaper, and had received clearance by the War Department. And the treatment of the local reporter, Trice, from the *Indianapolis Recorder*, has already been documented. Hunter somehow felt that the military had the power over the nation's press, and could do anything that they wanted. Whatever was the truth, the War Department did not want Hunter to have the final authority on press relations.

Hunter had been informed on several occasions that the War Department policy was to let the press on any station within the military. Gen. Giles told him again of this policy, but Hunter again resisted. "I don't mind them coming in, but I have command prerogatives to tell my base commanders that I don't want them to make any statements, and to refer them to me at my Headquarters." Giles had to make another try to get his attention. He pressed on, "Could you have your representative down there to make the statement that you wanted to make? I'm a little afraid the pressure's going to be so great we're going to be ordered to do it, if we don't let these boys on the station… because they'll say we've got facts we won't let out, we won't admit."

Giles was not successful in getting the message through to Hunter.

Hunter continued, "This *Chicago Sun* man called up my Intelligence people, and they told him I didn't have anything to do with it. By regulations, he had to clear it through the War Department. They all have to do that. We have kept none off the post who has been cleared through the War Department, but I don't want Selway making statements."

Hunter's interpretation of the rule was incorrect. If a reporter and his newspaper were cleared by the War Department, that reporter could go on any station anywhere in the world. But Gen. Hunter was a desperate man.

Giles told him he was wrong, "These boys have been cleared through the War Department."

Hunter finally got the idea, but he was not giving up. "Then they can go. I have no objection to their going on to the station, but I can control what my people say."

Giles made a small slip when he said, "Yes. Now that's what I want you to do. You can control exactly what you want Selway to tell them."

Hunter broke in again, "I don't want him to tell them anything. They're going to ask him all kinds of questions to put him in a very embarrassing position, and I'd rather handle that myself. I feel I'm better qualified."

Giles replied, "Well, could you have your press conference tomorrow, and go down there the day after tomorrow, and meet those boys there at that station, and clean it up."

"Are there any of them there?" asked Hunter.

"There are two or three of them there. I know one fellow, he's been there a week, right in the town, waiting to get in and he's raising hell up here…" Hunter's feathers began to droop, but he gave it one more try, "Well, if we notify them that I'm having this conference here tomorrow, you don't think they…the day after tomorrow… you don't think they'll come to that? I haven't got time to have it tomorrow."

His patience finally at an end, Giles let him have it straight from the shoulder. "Monk, the boys here from the War Department Bureau of Public Relations recommend that you let them on. They recommend that you make a statement, and then either you or your agent, or you instruct Selway to make a statement, nothing more. They don't answer a damned question. They do nothing. This is a statement, and I think it would be a good idea to let those newspaper boys go look these clubs over. Show what the Negroes had, show what they're fussing about. In fact, they had better club facilities than the white officers had. That probably will help the case. Selway will not have to answer questions of any kind. He only reads a statement that you will tell him to read, and that's all. You tell him to keep his mouth shut other than that. He doesn't answer one question. He makes a prepared statement and gives it to them."

Hunter had just received a royal "chewing out" by a three-star general.

He simply replied, "All right."

Giles, reaching an all-time low in what the white man will do in the fight to continue segregation, had a specific suggestion.

"Now, I'd recommend that you let those boys… let Selway show them just what he showed me, and also let them talk, if they want to, to this senior colored man. I don't know whether that would be advisable or not, but that senior colored man down there… it would be a good idea to let the press talk to Hayes because he said that the Negroes were absolutely 100 percent wrong."

It seems that there was always one black that would do what was wanted by the whites. In fact, it would appear that was how Hayes reached the rank of major.

At this, Hunter showed a stroke of genius. "Suppose they want to talk to some other. I advise against it because it's going to stir up trouble, I can tell you that right now." Giles agreed, "The thing is to have Selway give them a prepared written statement, and not answer any questions, and not let anyone else be queried. I think that will cover it."

"All right."

"And you can brief Selway on what to let them have, and then that will get the boys off our necks here. The Secretary of War figures probably we've got something we're trying to cover up."

The Secretary was right, of course.

Hunter, feeling somewhat better, began to sum up his approach. "Barney, my statement is going to be a very short and straightforward statement. It's going to be that, as far as I'm concerned, this is purely a question of military administration and discipline. Now, I am not passing on the legal aspect, the legality of the orders I issue. That is for a higher authority to pass on. Those orders were approved by me, that Selway was my agent, and I approved his orders, and his allocation of officers clubs."

As the conversation came to a close, Hunter felt that he was being understood somewhat, that they both knew they were trying to justify their acts.

Giles, being helpful, added, "And you closed the Club to avoid a riot."

"All right, I wasn't going to put that in the statement. If you want that…"

"I think it's a good idea to put that in, because I personally believe it did avoid a riot." *Again, the violence theme.*

"Oh, yes, there's no question about that. I hate to acknowledge that we have to close the clubs because we're afraid of them."

"'Of course, they do know the reason for it. Well, the military commander… it's always within his prerogative to do anything he wants to in case of riot or emergency. When will you have your statement prepared? I'd like to get one of these sharpshooters down here that have been in this business for a long time to come up there and talk to you about it."

Giles gave Hunter final clearance to hold a press conference, with some restrictions: "You can make a press conference on it. Of course, we want to get together and be very careful. How about sending one of these hotshots up there to talk with you tomorrow, to prepare a statement? Then have that sent on down to Selway, what he's to say, then check pretty well with what you're to give them, because this is a hot potato down here right now—somebody's already taken it to President Truman—and we want to be sure that we're all together on it."

As the conversation continued there was more evidence that Hunter was, as usual, behind the curve on events. Giles had just finished telling Hunter that President Truman was informed about the events. I do not believe that Hunter understood where President Truman stood on the question of fairness to blacks in the armed forces. Had he understood, he would have known why Gen. George C. Marshall, Chief of the Armed Forces, the highest military authority in the nation, was on his case.

Hunter continued, "I've ordered Selway… I didn't want to release those people until I could give them their reprimands, but General Walsh called me up and said General Marshall wanted to make a release to the press that they had been released from arrest, so I called up Selway and told him to have them released today, and tomorrow we'll get the reprimands out to them. I'm having Selway address a reprimand to each one of them, and I'm using word for word the reprimand that Ray Owens sent down here, prepared by Hedrick. I think it's splendid."

Hunter carried on, "There's one other thing. I'm adding a third paragraph on this: 'You will acknowledge receipt of this by endorsement hereon.' Now if they refuse to acknowledge receipt of that, then that will be something else." In a conspiratorial tone, the two got it together. Giles replied, "That's right, it really will be something else."

"They've refused already to answer that, but I'm going to give it to them again."

"Let them have it again… with both barrels. Okay, Monk."[61]

12

Release Of the 101

Gen. George C. Marshall, Chief of Staff of the Army, most likely having received his order directly from President Truman, in turn gave Gen. Giles the order to release us, the mutinous 101 under house arrest at Godman Field. Giles passed this order on to Gen. Hunter. Upon receiving the order, Hunter was upset, and looked for some way he could add further injury.

The release order did not stipulate that we should or should not be punished. Had the order included a provision that we should be released without punishment, everything would have been fine. Hunter used the loophole to give each officer an administrative reprimand. He chose this type of reprimand because it would remain in each officer's official military record, the 201 File. On the other hand, punishment under the 104th Article of War would have expired within a specified period of time, and would be removed from an officer's record. In addition, under the provisions of Article of War 104, we could have accepted or refused punishment and demanded trial by court-martial. Since the order (AR 85-2) was illegal, any trial based on the order would have been unsuccessful. Again, Hunter had taken advantage of a situation to have his own way.

I do not have a copy of my endorsement, but, according to Charles L. Francis's book, *The Tuskegee Airman,* in reply to this reprimand several officers submitted the following letter:

"For the record, the undersigned wishes to indicate over his signature his unshakable belief that racial bias is Fascist, un-American, and directly contrary to the ideals for which he is willing to fight and die. There is no officer in the Army who is willing to fight harder, or more honorably for his country and the command, than the undersigned. Nor is there an officer with a deeper respect for the lawful orders of superior authority.[62]

"The undersigned does not expect or request any preferential treatment for the tenure of his service, but asks only protection of his substantial rights as a soldier and as an individual, the same identical opportunities for service and advancement offered all other military personnel, and the extension of the identical courtesies extended all other officers of the Army."[63]

On April 23, 1945, we were, in fact, released from arrest, although the three officers accused of jostling the Officer of the Day continued to be held. To a man, the released officers made a "mad dash" to Louisville for some much needed recreation at our unofficial officers club at 13th Street and Magazine, known as "Dave's Bar." The club was alive that night. The Louisville ladies would only entertain the men who had been under arrest. Interestingly, there were many more in attendance who had been "arrested" than the actual 101.

13

On A Different Track

On May 31, 1945, Gen. Born, Commanding General, Continental Air Force, informed Gen. Glenn that a directive had been issued from HQ AAF, and approved by the Secretary of War, that every effort would be made to make the 477th Bomb Group purified, in all positions. The term "purified" simply meant that the Group would be made all-black in every position. Gen. Born was very specific: "If you haven't sufficient officers in your own First Air Force, they will take all the officers needed from Tuskegee. The readiness date for the 477th Bombardment Group is changed from the first of July to the first of August. If you can't provide enough black officers to meet the needs of the Group, then you will fill the positions with white officers."

The ball had been thrown squarely into the lap of Gen. Arnold. Gen. Douglas MacArthur had stated that he would accept the 477th Bombardment Group in the Pacific Theater. Gen. Born emphasized the source of the directive with, "This decision has been handled at a high level right up to the Secretary of War."

More importantly, the status of the 477th Bombardment Group, and the problems that were being experienced by the Group, had reached President Truman. History has recorded President Truman's conviction that blacks should have a fair shake in the United States Armed Forces, especially the Army Air Force's flying programs. In 1938, Harry A. Truman, then a senator from Missouri, along with

Senator Everett Dirksen of Illinois, introduced an amendment to the original Civil Aeronautics bill for civilian pilot training guaranteeing that blacks would be able to participate in that program. It seems clear that when the arrest of the 101 black officers came to his attention, he made a decision favorable to the black officers of the 477th. *I would suggest that this is exactly what occurred.*

Gen. Glenn knew that Gen. Hunter would be mightily displeased and would resist the decision. He told Gen. Born, "General Hunter would positively recommend against it. He will say that the 477th will never be able to fight." Glenn knew that Hunter had done everything in his power to prevent the group from reaching combat-ready status.

Born reminded him, "If they get a directive that we would go, there is nothing that General Hunter can do."

Glenn experienced another bad moment. He pointed out that the 386th Service Group had entirely white officers. Born responded that "they were already aware of that fact." Glenn wanted something in writing to hang his hat on, but Born was reluctant to discuss that aspect with him. He did think he could get something in writing for planning purposes soon, though.[64]

This was the final, conclusive resolution of the 477th's problems. At last, the game was really over for the First Air Force. All decisions affecting the future of 477th Bombardment Group were now totally out of their hands. No doubt there was great anguish in FAF headquarters. All important decisions regarding the future of the 477th Bombardment Group would come from Headquarters Air Forces. More importantly, these decisions would be made without consulting Gen. Hunter. Previously, Hunter had been assured that before any definite directive or decision was made, he would be called in for conference to discuss the matter.

Hunter felt that because he had been involved with the group for over 18 months, he knew the situation better than anyone else. However, at that point in time, Headquarters Air Force was not interested. Hunter's racist feelings were too well known by the decision makers now in charge, and they knew any advice he had to offer would suffer from that racist point of view, and be of questionable validity.

On June 20, 1945, Col. Walter Urbach, OC/S, Continental Air Forces, called Gen. Glenn with more bad news for Hunter. Urbach informed Glenn that Continental Air Force had received instructions from Headquarters Army Air Force to make the 477th, the 387th, and the base squadron at Godman all colored. HQ had requested the assignment of Col. Benjamin O. Davis, Jr., the highest-ranking black officer in the Army Air Forces, to CAF for subsequent assignment to the FAF. HQ had also told him that they were proceeding with the procurement of the personnel designed to relieve the shortages made clear in various conferences.

Further instructions were provided to solve the so-called insurmountable difficulties anticipated in procuring utilities and personnel for Godman Field. Headquarters Army Air Forces had taken steps to transfer the responsibilities of utilities from AAF to Army Services Forces in order that the Commanding General of Fort Knox could take over the utility responsibilities; that is, the base engineer and the civilian operational support and funds.

Glenn's spirits dropped as he asked, "When would they receive the directive?" He was informed that he could proceed because the letter was in the mail. They were trying to give Hunter authority to make an appropriate announcement to the FAF personnel, though its contents would come from the War Department. Surely, Hunter was not eager to receive the information that USAAF Headquarters would

make the announcement. In fact, Gen. Eaker would probably make the announcement. Glenn could only say, "This
situation leaves First Air Force in an embarrassing predica-
ment not having this thing. It will appear practically as
though they have done nothing, and we haven't. Our hands
have been tied."

The announcement was going to be made at Godman
Field, and Col. Urbach suggested that Glenn or Hunter
might well be on hand. If so, it would take some heat off the
base. Glenn knew without a doubt that Hunter had specifically stated that he would prefer not to go.[65]

In fact, Hunter did not appear at Godman. Nor did
Glenn, for that matter. Instead, the two again threw Col.
Selway on the sacrificial fire. Selway would be the sole
representative of First Air Force at the change of command
ceremony.

On the June 21, 1945, Col. Benjamin O. Davis Jr.
assumed command of the 477th Bombardment Group and
Godman Field. The formal change of command did not take
place until the first of July.

If Hunter and HQ AAF thought that the problems with
the clubs was over, it was not. Gen. Anderson called Gen.
Glenn and informed him that a rumor had surfaced at
Godman Field that called Walterboro Air Base "dynamite."
The replacement training unit for the 477th was being
shipped to Walterboro in South Carolina, where there was
a "Jim Crow" Officers Club. Rumor had it that the black
officers planned to make a mass entry into the white club on
arrival at Walterboro with the idea of forcing decisive action
on the part of the War Department to wipe out "Jim Crow"
facilities at Walterboro, as well as to help prevent difficult
and serious misfortunes in the future. Anderson told Glenn
that Gen. St. Clair Streett had taken this information over to

Gen. Eaker. Streett just left the office here, and he wanted me to call you and suggest someone do something."[66]

As a results of these rumors, and wishing to head off any repeat of the Freeman Field Mutiny, Hunter got on the telephone to Col. Kirksey, Commanding Officer at Walterboro. "Guy, have you gotten Restricted Memorandum 600-45, War Department, 14th June?"

Kirksey wanted to know what it was all about. "It's about the command of Negro troops," shouted Hunter.

Kirksey thought he knew what Hunter was talking about. "Oh, that pamphlet."

But he was wrong, and Hunter told him so. "No, this is a change to the last paragraph of page 14 of the Pamphlet 20-6. It's on its way to you by the War Department, by order of the Secretary of War, signed by General Marshall. It means you can't have separate clubs. You can assign clubs by units, but if anybody wants to go in any other club, they can go. Now, this change, the distribution of it is to Commanding Officers, all Posts, Camps, and Stations in the United States."

Hunter continued, "Now, what I want you to do—it's ordered by the Secretary of War, and you have to obey it. Now, my suggestion is that you get all your white officers together, and caution them against losing their tempers or committing any overt acts. If the colored personnel come into your Club assigned to the white units, all they can do if they don't like it is to get up and go out. If it looks like you're going to have serious trouble, you'll have to make the decision whether, to prevent serious trouble, you will close both Clubs. Do you understand?"

Kirksey allowed as how he did understand, but that he had some reservations.

Hunter reminded him again to caution the white officers against any overt acts. He even suggested that if the white officers did not want to eat in the same mess, that Kirksey could get a house off base, and set up his own mess off base.

Hunter evidently had finally gotten religion. He even went so far as to read AR 210-10 Paragraph 19 to Kirksey, and said that Kirksey could assign facilities for use of particular military units, but that such assignments could not result in the exclusion on the basis of race or color. During this conversation, he advised Kirksey at least four times to get his white officers together, and caution them not to do anything foolish.

However, Kirksey did not give up. He asked if he could suggest that the blacks go to their own club and mess. Hunter advised him that "he could not do that because it was contrary to this memorandum, and they (the black officers) got the Secretary of War behind them."

"Keep me advised if you have any trouble that you can't handle," Hunter said.[67]

What a pity that such a clarifying memorandum had not been issued before these commanders had begun the segregation actions on those clubs at Selfridge Air Base.

14

Col. Davis Takes Command

On June 30, 1945, Gen. Hunter's Chief of Staff, Gen. Glenn, called Col. Benjamin O. Davis, Jr. at Godman Field. This was the day before the official change of command. Although Davis had assumed command on June 21, the change-of-command ceremony did not take place until the first of July.

This conversation was remarkable on many levels. To the casual reader many years later, or to the uninitiated, the discussion between Glenn and Davis appears innocent enough. To those of us who were involved in the events of the day, Glenn's conduct represents yet one more effort to diminish and demean the officers of the 477th.

It is important to understand that Glenn was Davis' superior by a single grade, and that Davis had come to this assignment from two years' experience as a combat commander in Italy. Nevertheless, throughout the conversation Glenn consistently manifested a paternalistic, demeaning, patronizing, and insulting attitude toward Davis. Remarkably, when Glenn turned to the coming court-martial, he even presumed to instruct Davis, an experienced West Point graduate, in military customs and decorum.

Glenn was treating a West Point graduate and veteran combat commander as if he were a new company commander and newly-promoted Captain, rather than an experienced commander.

To Davis' credit, he, of course, remained his usual unflappable self. Glenn's condescending attitude could not have been lost on Davis, but his replies were marked by a dignity equal to his coolness under fire.

The significance of this phone call, with all its nuances, can better be established by quoting it at length. Read it carefully.

This is the form that was used in the official transcript:

Gen. G: I wanted to call you just before you take over command down there, and find out if you are thoroughly satisfied that you are ready to take over.

Col. D: Yes, Sir, I believe so. We are going to have a few difficulties, but I think things are going to go along all right.

Gen. G: I know you are going to have some difficulties; we are cognizant of that . You have a terrific job, and I know you will have some difficulties, and I still mean what I told you before if we can assist you or cooperate with you in any way. We want to be kept informed. I wanted to call you also and tell you effective tomorrow, when you take over, midnight, if you are ready to take over at that time, your channels of command, you know, will be through here to higher headquarters. I want to emphasize that so you will know about it. One other thing I wanted to tell you about, you are having Monday a courts-martial, the first of its kind, and the first one you have had there, and the Commanding General and all of us are going to be watching the thing. A lot of people are. You, as president of the court, will be entirely responsible in charge for running it. There is one thing I want to emphasize to you, though, for you to make certain that it's conducted with the customary military dignity.

Col. D: I will certainly do that, General.

Gen. G: The reason I emphasize that is… I don't know if you are going to have photographers there or not, but, as a rule, the smashing of bulbs and flash lights and all that in a court makes more of a travesty of it—it lacks dignity in a military court.

Col. D: I have decided that would not be in keeping with the dignity of the court.

Gen. G: I am not trying to influence you at all, because it will be entirely up to you, but I'm glad you have made that decision.

Col. D: We have already made that decision.

Gen. G: Fine. One other thing. On your press relations we have a number of policies within the FAF which are all based on War Department policies. I don't know whether you are familiar with them or not. You have just been overseas, and I know when I came back, there were many things in policy here in the states that I had lost touch with entirely. There is one thing, though, I want you to watch out for, and that is the matter of any controversial matters on racial matters, etc. We don't publish those, or give those out to the press on any of our bases. Watch your step on that.

Col. D: I will certainly do that.

Gen. G: I know you will. I can't think of anything else. Tell your public relations officer—I assume you have one—and anything that is issued in the way of press, of course, should be issued under your name. At least you are responsible for it. You understand that?

Col. D: Yes, Sir. There is one thing in that connection. I understand from him that anything for national release goes through your headquarters.

Gen. G: Here is the dope on that. The War Department requires that before you can put out anything for national release or even admit correspondents or representatives of national organizations, magazines, etc., who have a nation-wide coverage, that has to be approved by the War Department. We want those done, to submit your request to us. It will be forwarded to the War Department immediately, but it merely lets us know what is going on. The Associated Press is in the same category. We had a court-martial here the other day, and we had representatives of the *New York Times*, Associated Press, etc., and that all had to be approved in Washington, with their concurrence. I was a little concerned on this release that Ming put out direct to the War Department Bureau of Public Relations that, of course, the Judge Advocate is a little bit out of his line, and that went straight to the War Department Bureau of Public Relations from your place.

Col. D: That went through Captain McIntosh.

Gen. G: Yes, I know it did, and he in turn failed to clear it through Col. Selway. That is not your fault. As long as he took it up with his intelligence section, why, that's "hunky-dory." Not your fault at all. They were entirely to blame for it, but those things, of course, should come through here. You understand the regular channels. In regard to training, etc., are you having any troubles that we can help you with?

Col. D: No, Sir, not right now. As you undoubtedly know, I have already made two squadrons out of the four.

Gen. G: I assumed you would, based on that General Order that we put out authorizing the deactivation of the other two.

Col. D: We don't have that yet. I sure would like to have it. That is exactly what I was leading up to. I do need that.

Gen. G: We have issued the order for the activation of the composite group, the activation of the 99th, the deactivation of two squadrons, and activation of the other one.

Col. D: That is what we need right now, and I don't have that yet.

Gen. G: It cleared out of here about three days ago. If you haven't gotten it, I better put it on TWX and shoot it to you.

Col. D: I would appreciate that, General.

Gen. G: I will get it on the way for you. Anything else?

Col. D: Just this other thing, and that is to request that when we make requests for officers, that HQ higher than yours realize the importance of getting them here because of the shortage at hand.

Gen. G: What we do on that, if we get the request here, we generally, on the long distance telephone, handle it, and if you have shot in any of those and you are not getting prompt action, let me know.

Col. D: All right, Sir, I will do that. Thanks very much.[68]

After the FAF's record of training this group, an offer of assistance in training is similar to the captain of the Titanic *giving advice on how to avoid icebergs.*

The 477th Reborn

After Col. Davis assumed command, capable black officers assumed the positions of responsibility that had been denied them so long, and morale began to recover.

Davis set about getting the group ready for combat, and overcoming the inexcusable job of training by his predecessor. He deactivated two squadrons, the 619th and the 616th. He retained the 617th and 618th, and transferred the 99th from Walterboro to Godman. The former four-squadron bomb group became a three-squadron composite group—two bomber squadrons and a fighter squadron.

15

The Trial

A total of 162 black officers were arrested at Freeman Field
for refusing to sign a statement that they had read Base
Regulation 85-2. In response to widespread nationwide
indignation and protest, the War Department directed that
all but three be freed—58 were released at Freeman, 101 at
Godman. Separate charges against these three were based on
their alleged conduct the first night of the mutiny at the
Officers Club Number Two.

The trial[69] of the three officers was, in a sense, anticli-
mactic. Nevertheless, recounting of the highlights of the trial
shows clearly the extent that the Army Air Forces continued
to press the issue of segregation and discrimination. The
efforts of Col. Selway and Gen. Hunter to destroy the 477th
Bombardment Group have been documented in the previous chapters. The trial testimony provides still another
demonstration of the deceit and stultifying racism of these
commanders.

The General Court-Martial trial of Lts. Roger Terry,
Marsden Thompson, and Shirley Clinton was unique in
several ways. It was the first court-martial ever scheduled on
an army base commanded by a black commander. Second,
it was the first trial in the United States Army where the
board consisted totally of black officers, although an earlier
list reported to the Secretary of War recommended that "the
Trial Judge Advocate, Defense Counsel, and five of the nine
members be colored, and suggested that this proportion be

followed in the composition of the court-martial when it is convened." However, the most significant factor is the indefensible nature of the court-martial itself. This court-martial should have never been convened. There should have never been a trial!

A number of Air Force internal memoranda make clear that the charges should not have been carried to court-martial. One of the most telling memos came from Col. R. E. Kunkel, Chief of the Military Justice Division at Headquarters Army Air Forces. Among his observations were the following: "This office is informally advised by the office of the Air Judge Advocate that all Combat Crew Training personnel at the field are Negroes, there being no white trainees, and no Negro officers other than trainees. It thus appears that as a practical matter, the only officers prohibited from entering that particular Officers Club were Negro officers.

"Trial by court-martial of these officers could, it is believed, raise question of racial discrimination, since it appears that the only officers excluded from the Officers Club in question were Negro officers. Particularly would this be so if these officers should be charged with violation of Article of War 64, a capital offense. Such action would probably result in wide, and probably unfavorable, publicity. Under these circumstances, I am of the opinion that although these officers were probably guilty of infractions of discipline, that long-range public interest does not appear to warrant a trial by courts-martial on charges growing out of the incident described. Further, there is the unlikelihood that, at such a trial, the accused would receive sentences involving dismissal from the service or such if sentences were adjudged that they would be confined. Examination of the Report of Investigation submitted by the Inspector General discloses that he concurs in the conclusions reached therein, one of which states that the conduct of these mentioned officers, who allegedly used force in obtaining entrance to the club, was so flagrant and lacking in mitigating circumstances that its recognition as a major offense is mandatory. Then the report recommended that no further action in this case be taken. However, for the preservation of military discipline, and the desired deterrent effect on future occurrences of this nature, as well as the necessity for apprising others that obedience of orders is essential to the proper functioning of the Army, it is thought that the conduct of these three officers should not be entirely overlooked." In short, Kunkel suggested that Thompson, Clinton, and Terry ought to face ordinary discipline from their unit commander, not court-martial.

Through most of June, HQ AAF remained unsure that the three should be court-martialed. Then the War Department issued an amendment to the directive wherein the Secretary of War directed that "appropriate disciplinary action be taken in the case, and that the action be expedited. This action does not preclude action under the 104th Article of War." This amendment was remarkably enlightened, except for the last sentence, which allowed Gen. Hunter discretionary power to choose the type of disciplinary action to be taken.

Hunter's mind was made up and he now had a free rein. He wanted a court-martial trial in the worst way. His first choice was to have court-martialed the entire group of arrestees, but since he had been denied that possibility, he set about court-martialing the three officers. On June 24, 1945, he issued Special Order Number 175, Paragraph 1, in which he appointed a General Court-Martial, and referred the matter to trial. The first part or the court-martial was to deal with the charges against Lts. Clinton and Thompson. Specifically, they were charged with "willfully disobeying a lawful command from Lt. Rogers, their superior officer."

The Trial of Lts. Thompson and Clinton Begins

It was a bright, sunny Monday morning, the second of July, 1945. The courtroom was military spit and polish. The flag of the United States hung at the proper angle, but seemed to have a sad droop, as if it were human and knew what was going on, and felt ashamed to be present. All else was ready for the trial. The court-martial Board, the precedent-shattering, all-black army court-martial was in place. Col. Benjamin O. Davis Jr., who had very recently succeeded Col. Robert R. Selway as Commander of the 477th Bombardment Group, had been appointed President of the Court-Martial Board by Hunter. This was certainly no task to be handed to the new black commander. As president of the Board, he was squarely in a position antagonistic to the officers and men of the 477th. Hunter would be watching his every move and ruling. Davis was in a no-win situation.

The courtroom was essentially sparse and plain. There was the long bench on a raised platform, for the Board to sit on, and two tables with straight chairs, for use by the defense and the prosecution, as well as chairs for the court reporter, Mr. John H. Goranflo, of Louisville, Kentucky, and the witnesses. There were minimal accommodations for spectators and the press.

On the bench, Col. Davis sat in the center. To his right sat Capt. George L. Knox, the senior Captain on the Board, and Capts. James T. Wiley, William T. Yates, and Fitzroy Newsum. On Davis' left was 1st Lt. William R. Ming, Jr., law member, the advisor to the court on the law. He was to interpret legal points which might arise. Ming was from

Chicago, where he was a former assistant attorney general for the State of Illinois. Next to Ming was Capt. John H. Durden, and other members of the Board, Capts. Charles R. Stanton, Elmore M. Kennedy, and James Y. Carter. James W. Redden and 1st Lt. Charles R. Hall were detailed as Trial Judge Advocates—that is, prosecutors—and Capt. Cassius A. Harris and 2nd Lt. William C. Coleman were the military defense counsels. 1st Lt. Edward K. Nichols had been appointed special counsel; however, he was confined to the post hospital at Fort Knox.

Thompson and Clinton were to be represented by civilian counsel. Since the NAACP had been engrossed in this incident since the beginning, it was now time for the legal department to take over. The Legal Defense Department was headed by Thurgood Marshall, and he selected two star defense lawyers to handle the defense. He asked the secretary of the Cincinnati branch of the NAACP, Theodore Berry, to head the defense team, assisted by Harold M. Tyler of the Chicago Branch.

With this high-power defense team on board, the accused dismissed the regularly court-appointed defense counsel, Capt. Cassius A. Harris III, who then was excused by the president of the Board, and withdrew from the court. However, Lt. William C. Coleman remained as an assistant to Mr. Berry.

The trial began. Neither the prosecution nor the defense challenged any member of the court for cause. However, both exercised their right to peremptory challenge. The prosecution challenged Capt. Charles E. Stanton. Stanton, a very fair-skinned Negro—"white as the next white man"— was excused from the board. *(Years later I met him in Japan, where it appeared that he was "passing" as a white. He has never been accounted for at any of the Tuskegee Airmen conventions or other functions.)* The defense made a peremptory challenge of Col. Davis and he, too, was excused from the Board.

The defense's challenge was both a small bombshell and a godsend.

It was a magnificent move, of great benefit to Davis, and to all black Army Air Force officers. Davis could not have been an effective leader of his men while at the same time sitting in judgment on some of them. Years later, in his biography, he did not remember the reason he was not on the Board. As with most events surrounding this story, there is controversy over how and why Davis was challenged. Bill Womack and Lawrence P. Scott, in their book, *Double V, the Civil Rights Struggle of the Tuskegee Airmen*, offered the following explanation:

"Prior to the trial, a few of the detailed court members allegedly met surreptitiously with the defense counsel for the three accused, and advised them to challenge, peremptorily, Davis' seat on the court. The officers who gave the advice feared that Davis, being a West Point man and an officer aspiring to be the first black general in the Air Force, might be disposed to find the accused guilty as charged, to save his career. The officers who disagreed with Davis' position felt that their careers would be in jeopardy. Those court members who owed their command responsibilities to Col. Davis feared that a favorable decision made by the court toward the three accused could cost Davis his career, as well as theirs. Either way, the officers felt that they could not afford to have Davis on the court."

Womack and Scott based this on an interview with Elmore Kennedy, a member of the court.[70]

This explanation of the rationale behind the challenge is flawed in that it concludes that the members of the Board were less concerned with the guilt or innocence of the accused than with their own future careers. This is simply insulting. It denigrates the integrity, not only of the officers on the board, but of the defense counsel, Theodore Berry.

In my recent telephone interviews with Col. James T. Wiley and Fitzroy Newsum, members of the court, both men denied that they had any knowledge of any such conversation or thoughts being expressed. They were very annoyed at this reckless statement.

With the withdrawal of Col. Davis, Capt. George Knox, the senior officer remaining on the Board, automatically became President of the Board.

The first witness was 1st Lt. Joseph D. Rogers. After being sworn in, he slowly turned and saluted the flag that was in the corner of the room. Shockingly, however, he refused to salute the President of the Board, as was customary in military trials. Knox stopped the trial, and glared at Rogers. In a deep voice edged with wrath, he reminded Rogers of the Army's custom, and waited. Slowly, Rogers turned, and saluted the court. This open disrespect was repeated by each white officer reporting to testify, including Col. Selway. Each time, Knox was required to stop the proceedings and remind the officer of the military court custom. In each case, after being reminded, each officer did reluctantly salute the court.

Rogers had considerable trouble when he was asked to relate to the court what order he had received, and how, from Provost Marshal Maj. Baumgardner. Especially difficult to recall were Baumgardner's instructions on how to recognized the non-member trainee officers to whom he should deny entry to the club. In the first place, he certainly did not want to talk about Baumgardner, since the Major had been fired from his duty as Provost Marshal for incompetent performance. The less said about him the better.

Berry would have liked to have elicited the truth. The most likely words of Baumgardner to Rogers probably went something like this: "Rogers, you go over to that club and tell any 'nigger' that tries to enter that he can't, and if he insists on entering, you arrest his ass, you hear?" Rogers, of course, knew that would present enormous difficulty for him, and to say these words would create immense problems for his superiors.

Nevertheless, Berry had to try for the truth. He asked Rogers, "Will you state in as near exact words as you can recall the exact instructions Major Baumgardner gave you?" Rogers immediately got into trouble. He simply answered that he was told to keep trainee personnel and non-members out of the club. The obvious question in everyone's mind was how would he be able recognize these personnel. The prosecution knew, as did Rogers, that this was going to be a difficult question. The obvious answer was that if they were black, they were trainees.

"How did you recognize the officers who approached the club as trainees?" Berry asked. Rogers struggled for an answer. First he tried the fact that the men wore wings, but it must have crossed his mind that nearly 90 percent of all male officers on the base wore wings, including white personnel, instructors, and supervisors. This distinction alone would not separate these officers as trainees. When asked who wore pilot wings, he answered that he did not know. Continuing to struggle, he weakly added that he recognized them from his own judgment.

Clearly Rogers was making a bad impression, as well as suffering obvious confusion. It got worse when he admitted that he did not ask for any identification. He simply told the men to stop so he could tell them that they could not enter the building. He did this without asking them if they were trainees or not. The only conclusion that could be drawn from his testimony to this point was that the only criterion that he used to determine that these men were trainees was they were black. Under further questioning Rogers admitted that he did not know how any members of the club were identified upon entering the club.

The prosecution's next witness was the Club Officer, Maj. White. White was the officer who placed the 61 officers under arrest during the initial two days of the unrest on April 5 and 6. White seemed to lose his ability to recall the events of that night as his time in the witness chair increased. When asked if one of the officers asked him why they should leave, he could not recall ever being asked that question. But he did recall that he placed the entire group in arrest. His reason was that none of them made an attempt to leave the club. He also said that he "knew none of them was a member because he, as Club Officer, controlled the books." Yet, he did not ask any of the officers their names, which he said "was not necessary because he knew all the club members by name."

White continued to give strange answers to questions that told of his mind-set that night. He claimed that he had not been given any orders to exclude any officers from the club, yet he was ordering officers out of the club. The reason was, as he stated, "because they were non-members." Yet, he did not inquire if they wished to become members.

When Capt. Anthony Chiappe, the white Commander of Squadron E, was called, he testified that he was not a member of the club; yet, he was there enjoying all the amenities of a member. No one had questioned his member-ship when he entered the club.

He claimed to have called a meeting of all the officers on the following morning. I personally know that I never attended a meeting of the officers of the 118th called by

Capt. Chiappe. The officers' mess that the black officers used was separate from the one combined with the club that Chiappe mentioned.

One additional significant question was asked of Chiappe: "Did any of the men, either singly or collectively, ask you the question whether this was a club exclusively for white officers, and, if so, what was your reply?" Chiappe allowed as how he did not remember his answer, nor did he remember if he told the officers which Officers Club they were supposed to use.

After being asked several more questions, at which times he displayed a complete loss of memory and gave the answers that he did not remember or could not recall, Chiappe was excused.

Testimony Of Col. R. R. Selway

After a short recess, the court turned to Col. Selway, who also refused to salute the court until reminded by Capt. Knox. Almost immediately, his testimony became very interesting. Not only was he a very hostile witness, but he seemed to be in deep denial of many of the known facts. Several times during his testimony he made the statement, "I think these questions are objectionable, irrelevant, and immaterial. I think this entire line of questioning is irrelevant."

Selway repeatedly denied the responsibility of all directives and letter orders. He denied any knowledge of having issued any orders or memoranda prior to April 5, 1945, when, in fact, at that very time he was pleading with Gen. Hunter to know if "his orders were legal." These were the memoranda and orders that were being read to the black officers at the direction of Hunter, designed to segregate the Officers Clubs at Freeman Field.

The fireworks began when the defense questioned Selway about the orders and memoranda he gave to Lt. Col. Pattison to read to the officers at the theater on March 10, 1945. Selway immediately denied any association with orders that gave directions about the use of the Officers Club Number Two. He said he believed "there was a regulation issued around the first of the month under the name of my predecessor, Col. Bradford; he had been Station Commander." Selway claimed Pattison had received instructions to go over there, and read that and explain it. "I have no written record of the oral instructions or information I gave to him." Selway suggested that he was not sure of the subject matter of the regulation, or what memorandum the defense was talking about. He further explained that Pattison, in conference, "made certain notes on the instructions I issued to him orally. There was no written memorandum; it was his memorandum, I suppose, trying to remember what to say."

This denial by Selway was unconscionable. He denied knowledge of the very documents that he had discussed in detail with Gen. Hunter on the telephone with great clarity. During that conversation on March 10, 1945, Selway declared that he was going to close the Club until he could find out if his order was legal. The night before, on March 9, 1945, two groups of black officers had entered the Club, but were declined service, and they departed. Hunter ordered Selway, "You get your key people in and give them the orders, and they can get those orders right down to those troops. Any of them that do not comply with orders, and I'll back you as long as you've got that thing divided that way according to regulations, and that's the way it is." Hunter further stated, "I want your orders enforced. Any individual insubordination, or mass insubordination, I want them put in close arrest, and I want to know about it right away."

Again, Selway wanted to check his orders. He pleaded to Hunter. "I want to check my orders and, if it's legal, then I'm going to slap them in arrest and trial, but I wanted to check my orders to see if they had been misinterpreted."

Selway was confident that the defense did not know about these telephone calls. He could lie without risk of being found out. He was intensely involved in blocking the black officer's use of Officers Club Number Two. When asked if he was aware that any officers of color were denied admission to Mess and Officers Club Number Two, he replied, "Again this is all hearsay, and not through my own knowledge. I was never present when any person was denied that."

His calling Hunter and threatening to close the Club because black officers had entered, and would with all probability visit the Club again soon, was by no means hearsay.

Continuing to attack in the same area, defense called a number of black officers that had been involved in the incident. 2nd Lt. Robert Payton testified that he was not admitted to the Officers Club Number Two, and was told by Maj. White that colored officers at that time were not admitted. 2nd Lt. Coleman A. Young, who had been one of the major leaders of the black officers, provided other details.

Young testified that as Thompson went into the Club, Rogers grabbed and pushed him. Young said Rogers turned and grabbed and pushed Thompson, pushed him to the side. "I also saw Rogers push Clinton as he entered the Club. Rogers followed Thompson in the door, Clinton and the rest of us followed Thompson and Rogers. He was quite close— not more than three feet separated us. In fact, I was right behind him. After Rogers walked away towards the rear of the Club, the group of us who had entered moved into various parts of the Club. I went to the bar and asked for a beer."

Young was not served; the bartender said he had instructions not to serve non-members. He asked the bartender how could he tell whether or not someone was a member? The bartender explained that "no colored men belonged to the Club." Young did not hear Maj. White tell Thompson or Clinton to leave the Club, but he did hear Maj. White tell them, "If you refuse to leave, I will have to arrest you." The Major then asked Young, "What is your name?" and placed him under arrest.

2nd Lt. Clifton, 2nd Lt. Clarence Garrett and F/O Howard Story followed as witnesses, and added little new information. It is important to note that Garrett was with Payton, and testified to White's statement: "I might as well be frank about it. I have orders not to admit any colored personnel in the Club." Garrett also testified that Rogers did shove Thompson.

Story corroborated Garrett's testimony: "As I said before, Lt. Thompson was the first in, and I saw Lt. Rogers put his hand on him to keep him from going into the Club—he was already in the Club. Then, after he got in, he put his hand on Lt. Thompson, and I believe I heard Lt. Thompson say, 'Take your hands off of me, Lieutenant,' or something to that effect." Story added that Rogers went over to Clinton as he was coming in the Club and turned around to stop him, and he pushed him back.

The testimony of the two accused officers is important in certain aspects, although most of the questions by the court were almost the same, since they dealt with the same events. Clinton did clarify the question about the entry doors into the Club. There were two doors and two screen doors that opened outward. The defense wanted to know if, in opening the door, this could have hit Rogers. Clinton said that it could not have, because the door opened outward, and Rogers was already in the Club.

Clinton did not believe that at any time did Rogers say anything that could have been considered as an order from a superior officer to do or not to do anything. In fact, he gave no orders at all.

Lt. Thompson testified that he went to the Club alone, and did not have any conversation with anyone until he arrived at the door, where he encountered Lt. Rogers. "As I approached the Club I saw a group of men standing around talking—they was saying something about what had happened or something like that, so I didn't pay much attention to them. I was in a hurry. I wanted to make this phone call, and I walked up to the door, and walked in the Club and, just as I stepped in the Club one or two paces, I was met by Lt. Rogers. Rogers said, 'This Club isn't for you fellows.' And I said, 'Why isn't it for us fellows?' and he said, 'Well, Lieutenant, if you will step outside, I will explain it to you,' so I stepped outside, and there were quite few other fellows coming up at the same time. So, he said, 'This is a Base Officers Club,' and Lt. Clinton put in and said, 'I am a Base Officer. Why am I not allowed to go in the Club?' and he said 'I can't answer that,' and I just walked on in when he said that, and he came in behind me and pushed me by the arm over to the side, and I said, 'Lieutenant, take your hands off of me,' and at that time—it was a matter of seconds— Clinton was right behind me, and Rogers went over to stop Clinton, and after he left me, I started into the Club—there were quite a few other fellows who came in behind us."

At the conclusion of Thompson's testimony, and after some final legal wrangling, the defense rested. Following a short recess for deliberation and secret ballot, the decision for Clinton and Thompson was announced:

"Of all specifications and charges: Not Guilty."

The Trial begins for Terry

On July 3, 1945, at 1:00 p.m., the trial of Lt. Roger C. Terry began. His long nightmare was about to come to an end or become a reality, depending on the outcome of the trial. He had not been officially notified of the Thompson/Clinton verdict, but was aware that they had been found not guilty. More importantly, he knew that there was a good chance that the "Army's man, the military ramrod with that West Point background," Col. Davis, would not be on the court-martial board.

This trial would not be much different from that of Thompson and Clinton; however, the charges against Terry were more extensive. In addition to the charge of willfully disobeying a command from Rogers (as were Thompson and Clinton), Terry was also accused of "offering violence against Lt. Rogers." Most of the witnesses and the testimony in Terry's trial duplicated and paralleled those in Clinton's and Thompson's.

However, the defense added as witnesses Lt. James V. Kennedy, the officer who was with Lt. Terry, and Capt. Franklin A. McLendon, Special Services Officer of the 477th.

When the court met, neither the prosecution nor the defense had any challenges for cause, but the prosecution again challenged Capt. Stanton peremptorily, and the defense again challenged Col. Davis peremptorily. Capt. George Knox again assumed the Presidency of the Board.

Lt. Terry immediately made clear that he did not desire the services of the regularly-appointed defense counsel, Capt. Cassius A. Harris. Instead, he wished to be defended by the regularly-appointed Assistant Defense Counsels, Lt. William C. Coleman and 1st Lt. Edward K. Nichol—

known as "Slick Nick" because of his skill in military trials. Terry also selected Special Defense Counsel Theodore M. Berry.

The first witness called was Rogers, who testified that he stopped the three officers (Kennedy must have caused Rogers some moments of confusion; in appearances Kennedy looked more white than did Rogers), and told them that they could not enter the building, and when they seemed inclined to enter anyway, he gave them an order not to enter the building. He was not exactly sure how he gave the order, but finally stated that he said, "This is a direct order; you can't enter this building." Rogers added that Terry reached down to his right and pushed him out of the way so Terry could get at the doorknob. Terry pulled the door open and pushed him further to the side with the door, and that Terry and the other two officers entered the building.

Under cross-examination, Rogers became confused about whether he was alone, as he had stated in a certificate he executed three days after the incident. He now testified that Lts. Harrison and Rice were with him at the time of the incident. After riding this out, there came the matter of identification of the officers, a matter he had a problem with during the first trial. Again, he fell back on the answer that he had used in the first trial—it was a matter of his own judgment. He admitted that he had not stopped or restrained any white officers who approached the Club that night.

As it turned out, Rogers had contradicted his own statement, given just three days after the incident, which made clear that he had not given any order direct or otherwise, not to enter the Club. He had originally indicated that he was alone, but later testified that he had been joined by two other white officers, one who was wearing a side arm.

In fact, Terry, Kennedy, and Goodall were confronted by three white officers, two who were armed, all with the intention of preventing their entry into the Officers Club. These lieutenants, Rice and Harrison, were both assigned to the Provost Marshal's office, and they testified almost exactly the same as Rogers. They had both been relieved from duty as Provost Marshals at the same time as had Maj. Baumgardner.

The next prosecution witness, Capt. McLendon, testified that he was inside the Officers Club and, although he could not hear all the conversation between Terry and Rogers, he did see all the action. He stated, "I would not say it was rough or anything like that, but I would say Lt. Terry merely pushed Lt. Rogers from the door because he was standing with his back to the door, and he reached around and got the knob of the door, and opened the door, and he went inside. After they got inside, if I remember correctly, the Club Officer, that was Major White, he was called… that happened just inside the door… Major White just came up and told the officer, he said, 'You men will be placed under arrest,' or words to that effect, or 'You men are now under arrest.' He said, 'I will have to take your names,' and at that time he took his paper and pencil and took the names of the men—they were willing to give their names, and they all gave their names, and after they gave their names they then went out orderly. That is all I know about it."

The defense called Col. Robert R. Selway as its first witness.

During his testimony Selway insisted, as he had in the previous trial, that all questions asked were irrelevant and immaterial. His answers, at times, were simply amazing in light of the information contained in the record to the contrary. For instance, when he was asked: "Were you at that time familiar with Army Regulation 210-0, Paragraph 19?" he replied, "I don't like to take the Court's time, but I want to state in here that I am objecting to every question and answer—I want it entered in the record I am objecting to every question on the grounds they are irrelevant and immaterial."

At this point, the Law Member interrupted and proceeded to chastise Selway. "The right to object to questions is the right of counsel, and not the right of the witness." Selway continued to object, but the Law Officer had the last word. "The witness has no right to object to questions."

The Defense Counsel made the only statement necessary, "In light of the Colonel's statement I should like to ask the Court to consider this witness as a hostile witness." The Law Member agreed, "Subject to objection by any member of the Court, the Law Member will rule that the Defense Counsel is entitled to treat the witness as a hostile witness."

Selway knew that this trial was not solely about these three black officers and their alleged conduct. This trial was about him and his policies. As J. Alfred Phelps succinctly stated in *Chappie*: "It was his regime and tactics that were on trial... so of necessity, he had to be very hostile... He was the one being defied. He was simply the organization man... He was carrying out the orders. As such, he would not have learned anything. All he knew was rigidity... do as we tell you... apply the segregation system. He never learned anything. There was no way in the world he'd back off his position."

Continuing his testimony, Selway gave answers that were in character to his hostility. He did not feel that the effect of the order restricting the black officers to the use of certain buildings, particularly Officers Club Number Two, resulted in discrimination against the officers of color under his command.

He instructed Maj. Baumgardner, "If he gave any direct orders to any personnel and they didn't obey them he would place them in arrest pending an investigation. Yet, I believed that the regulation was not negative or prohibitive in a sense."

He refused to answer the question, "Did you intend your order to restrict the use of Officers Mess and Club Number Two to white officers only?" Selway's interpretation of Col. Bradford's letter order shows his denial of the facts. He saw this order as a positive order designating the use of facilities, and could see no discrimination in it.

Berry continued to question Selway about the construction of the order, and Selway continued to insist that the order was merely designed to designate the facilities to be used by certain officers assigned to Freeman Field. Berry tried once again to pin Selway down to a specific building. "Was it your intention, when you adopted Colonel Bradford's order, to exclude any person from building T-930, Officers Club Number Two?" Selway replied, "Not for the reason you brought up. It was not my intention that anyone not be permitted to enter a public building."

Selway's testimony essentially consisted of the following: No officer was excluded from Officers Club Number Two. Any officers club on the base could be used by any officer, and, certainly, if the Commanding Officer on the base states that any officers club can be used by any officer, then an order to the contrary given by a subordinate would, on that basis, be out of order, if not illegal. Selway, continuing his denial, stated on cross-examination that "as Base Commander he knew of no order which excluded any officer from any officers club on the base." This testimony is certainly contrary to the evidence of the events of the mutiny.

Lt. James V. Kennedy, who was with Terry when they entered the Club, testified. Then, at his own request, Terry testified what happened as he entered the Officers Club Number Two. "As I went in, the Lieutenant, whom I later learned was Lieutenant Rogers, said, 'If you go in, you will be arrested.' Well, Lieutenant Kennedy and Flight Officer Goodall followed me in, and we made about three or four paces in the Club and we were met by a Major—Major White—he seemed to have been standing directly opposite the door as we came in. He came up and approached us with a pencil in his hand, and asked for our name and rank, and he told us we were to return to our quarters under arrest. On making that statement, Lieutenant Kennedy asked him why, and he said, 'I don't have to answer that, Lieutenant,' and, with that, we left."

After Terry's testimony, the trial concluded with the required formalities. The verdict was:

"Of Specification 1 (disobeying an order): Not guilty. Of Specification 2 (jostling a superior officer): Guilty. Of the Charge: Guilty."

Terry was sentenced to forfeit $50.00 per month for three months.

Gen. Hunter was outraged at Terry's sentence. In his mind it amounted to little more than a slap on the wrist. Hunter's endorsement to the trial reflected his anger and bitterness: "In the foregoing case of Second Lieutenant Roger C. Terry—the sentence, although grossly inadequate, is approved, and will be duly executed."

Epilogue

The 477th Bombardment Group came out of the Freeman Field mutiny strengthened. The mutiny did not win social equality for all black Army personnel, but it did result in black command of the 477th Bombardment Group. Its white command structure did not survive.

The reorganization was a victory for the courageous young black officers of the 477th. In the eyes of some people, this change merely represented increased segregation; to others it was a statement of freedom demonstrating that blacks could command and operate a bombardment group with all its demands and complexities. If we could not have rational integration, then radical segregation was a viable alternative.

On July 1, 1945, Col. Benjamin O. Davis, Jr., officially took command, and all white unit and base personnel were transferred. Key combat-experienced black officers joined the Group, and filled all the vacancies. After the court-martial, additional capable black officers assumed the positions of responsibility that had been denied them so long. Morale continued to improve.

Col. Davis had brought with him many veterans of the Italian campaign to augment the capable black officers already assigned to the Group. These officers included veterans Bill Campbell, Andrew "Jughead" Turner, Elmer Jones, Herbert Carter, Lee Rayford, Vance Marchbanks, Ed Gleed, and Thomas Money. The officers already with units of the 477th, who were elevated to command and staff positions, were Capt. C. I. Williams, command of the 617th

Bomb Squadron, Capt. Elmore Kennedy, command of the 618th Bomb Squadron, George Knox, Lott Carter, Hubert "Hooks" Jones, John Beverly, William Edelin, James Redden, Charles Stanton, George Webb, Carl Taylor, and many others.

With the departure of the white instructors and supervisors, many distasteful issues disappeared with them. However, many severe problems remained. A particularly galling frustration was the problem of providing housing for the officers and men that Col. Davis had installed as key personnel.

During Col. Selway's command, Fort Knox had been giving "47 sets of quarters to the officers stationed over there at Godman Field." Davis asked for 15, certainly a modest and reasonable request. Col. Throckmorton, the Post Commander at Fort Knox was rattled, and called First Air Force for advice:

"I don't know whether you are familiar with Fort Knox or not, but this is an old cavalry post. We have four General Officers living there on the post, and, by God, they just don't want a bunch of coons moving in next door to them. I mean leaving the colored question out of it, I have still got the very fine excuse that I've got several hundred of my own officers living off the post—men in key positions ***** I had a frank confidential talk with General Eaker, and he said, 'Well, actually, Throckmorton, I don't see why we are entitled to any quarters on your post."[71]

Davis' request was denied entirely for racial reasons. Davis stated in his autobiography that "as a result of this decision, all our married people, about 60 couples, were housed under extremely crowded conditions in two barracks buildings at Godman. The building Agatha and I lived in had two bathrooms for two floors full of people, and they had to devise a guard system to indicate whether the bathroom was being used by men or by women at any particular time. In both buildings, the rooms, which had been designed for single occupancy, were more like cells. In other buildings, they had been portioned off from one another with wooden panels that went only halfway to the ceiling, so there was no privacy.

"It was an absolutely disgraceful situation, and a terrible way to treat combat veterans who had fought one war and were soon to be on their way to fight another. I shall never forget nor forgive this nation and the armed forces this shameful treatment of our veterans and their families by officers of the U.S. Army, who were fully aware of the situation, and yet allowed it to continue. To add insult to injury, our palatial quarters were adjacent to barracks occupied by Italian prisoners of war under the control of the Fort Knox command.

"It took me a long time to absorb the effects of how the Fort Knox command treated our people. I remained livid with anger and frustration because of a situation that was beyond my ability to correct. I was responsible for the welfare of the unit, but we were living under appalling conditions I could not improve. I was mad at the world, and particularly mad at the U. S. Army. One thing helped me through this difficult time: I had a mission to perform, and I distracted myself by dealing with the myriad technical problems associated with getting the 477th ready for deployment."[72]

Godman was, as it had been since the 477th first arrived, a most inadequate air field for this group, and Col. Davis and the Air Force continued to attempt to find a more suitable base. In each case where an adequate base was found that would be ideal for the Group's needs, AAF also found that the Group was not welcomed by the citizens of the area.

The 477th continued at Godman and, with great intensity, began overseas training as a composite group consisting of two squadrons of B-25s—the 617th Bombardment Squadron and the 618th Bombardment Squadron, and one fighter squadron—the 99th Fighter Squadron, equipped with P-47 fighter aircraft.

Gen. Douglas MacArthur had accepted the bomb group for service in the Pacific Theater over the objection of Gen. Kenney, his Air Chief of Staff. As a composite group, we had received a definite mission of strafing in the invasion of mainland Japan. Our training missions were geared to this type of action. We were flying very low minimum-altitude, cross-country, and group-size formations doing line-abreast strafing gunnery missions. We were eager and ready to get on with the program. I had began to study maps of the route to Okinawa, as we would be ferrying our aircraft to that island.

Three weeks later, Gen. Hunter's liaison party made the report of Group Headquarters: "Operating very efficiently," and "Ready to function in combat as of this date." Of the two squadrons, the estimate was equally sanguine: maintenance was "excellent," morale was "very high," and both units "should be able to complete their training by August 31," readiness day, five weeks away.[73]

On August 14, three weeks later, the war was over.

Had a truly integrated organization been formed at the inception, even greater gains for blacks in aviation would have resulted. Had this reorganization taken place at Freeman Field, rather than at the dilapidated and inadequate Godman Field, this group would have had a much greater chance of succeeding.

The 477th remained a segregated unit after the war. Soon, the mission of the group changed from one of flying to one for discharging personnel who no longer desired to remain in the service . By mid-February 1946, the unit was reduced to 16 B-25s, 12 P-47s, 256 officers and 390 enlisted men.

On March 13, 1946, the 477th made what was to be its last move, going to Lockbourne Army Air Field, Ohio. Again, they had arrived in an area where they were not wanted. The editor of the *Columbus Citizen* opposed the unit's move to Lockbourne Field, just south of the city. Objecting to American "servants" doing the fighting for America, he labeled the 477th "a bunch of troublemakers," and wrote that he could prevent the move "if I really wanted to." He maintained that "this is still a white man's country." The relocation, however, was made.

Once there, the unit participated in war games, and flew proficiency and tactical missions. Throughout the year, the Group organized a public relations effort, entertaining the citizens of Ohio with shows, field days, fire power demonstrations, static displays, and other activities to better inform people about their flying mission. The 477th also participated in air shows and other aerial demonstrations elsewhere in the United States.

On July 10, 1947, the B-25s were deactivated after taking part in a combat exercise in central Georgia. The 477th Composite Group ceased to exist.

Appendices

Appendix A: Army Regulation 210-10, Paragraph 19

Paragraph 19 of Army Regulation 210-10 is one of the most significant Army regulations in the area of segregation. Yet, it is not based on race. It was written to ensure that all Army officers be admitted to all officers clubs on all stations, post or bases in the Army. However, it was used by Negro officers to fight segregation due to race.

This critical paragraph reads:

Use of public building by officers clubs, messes, or similar social organizations:

a. No officers club, mess, or other similar social organization of officers will be permitted by the post commander to occupy any part of any public building, other than the private quarters of an officer, unless such club, mess, or other organization extends to all officers on duty at the post the right to full membership, either permanent or temporary, in such club, mess, or organization, including the right equally with any and all other members thereof to participate in the management thereof, to hold office therein, and to vote upon any and all of the affairs thereof in which the officers concerned have an interest.

b. (1) Wherever permanent membership in any officers club, mess, or other similar social organization, with the right to acquire an interest in the permanent property thereof, in limited mess, or other social organization must, in order to be permitted to occupy any part of any public building other than the private quarters of an officer, extend the right of temporary membership to all officers on duty at the post and on such reasonable terms as to initiation fees, dues, and other charges as should be satisfactory to the temporary members.

(2) In the event of a disagreement as to the reasonableness of any such terms, the post commander will require the parties in disagreement to submit written statements of their respective views of the matter, and will forward the statements with his recommendations for the decision to the corps area commander, except that at exempted stations they will be forwarded to The Adjutant General for the decision of the Secretary of War.

Appendix B: Recreational Facilities

The Adjutant General's Office
Washington
AG 353.8 (3-5-43) OB-S-A-M   VED/ar-2B-939
March 10, 1943
SUBJECT: Recreational Facilities
TO: Commanding Generals, All Service Commands.
    Chief of Engineers.

1. Letter, SPX 353.8 (8-14-42) MS-SPOP-M,
August 15, 1942, subject, Recreational Facilities at Certain Posts, Camps and Stations,
is rescinded.

2. At posts camps and stations where the
garrison includes units of two or more races,
recreational facilities, including theaters
and post exchanges will not be designated for
any particular race.

3. Where necessary, recreational facilities
may be allocated to organizations in whole or
in part, permanently or on a rotation basis
provided care is taken that all units and
personnel are afforded equal opportunity to
enjoy such facilities.

    By Order of the Secretary of War:
    /s/ R.A. O'LEARY
    Adjutant General

    Copies furnished:
    Commanding General, Army Ground Force
    Commanding General, Army Air Force
    Commanding General, Services of Supply
    Division of the War Department General Staff
    The Inspector General
    Director, Special Service Division, SO
    Director, Military Personnel Division, SO

Appendix C: Base Regulation 85-2

The following is a copy of the now infamous Base Regulation 85-2:

```
HEADQUARTERS
FREEMAN FIELD
Seymour, Indiana
BASE REGULATION)              9 April 1945
NUMBER 85-2)
```

    ASSIGNMENT OF HOUSING
    MESSING AND RECREATIONAL FACILITIES FOR
    OFFICERS, FLIGHT OFFICERS AND WARRANT
OFFICERS

1. Army Air Force standards governing the control and curfew of personnel undergoing training, as differentiated from standards governing permanent party Base, Supervisory and Instructor personnel, authorize separate housing, messing and recreational facilities assignment to those to classes of personnel.

2. In compliance with orders from the Commanding General of the First Air Force, and according to Army Air Force standards as outlined in paragraph 1 above, the following assignments of housing, messing and recreational facility for Officers, Flight Officers and Warrant Officer is effective this date.

3. Flight Officer and Warrant Officer personnel undergoing OTU, Combat Crew and Ground and Air Replacement Training will use the housing quarters messing, recreational facilities as follows:

    BOQs and latrine Buildings
                        T-839 thru T-851
                        T-854 thru T-873
    Recreational Building   T-838

```
    Mess Building              T-837
    Club Building              T-835
    Tennis Courts              T-830
```
Base, Supervisory, Instructor and command
personnel will use the quarters, messing,
recreational facilities as follows:

```
    BOQs, VOQs, Latrine Building
                 T-913 thru T-929
                 T-932 thru T-934
                 T-936 thru T-951
                 T-1050 thru T-1055
    Recreational Building      T-935
    Mess Building              T-930
    Club Building              T-930
    Tennis Courts              T-880
```

4. Personnel undergoing OTU, Combat Crew and
Ground and Air Replacement Training are de-
fined as Follows:

a. Personnel assigned to the 477th Bomb
Group (M), except those officially designated
as assigned for Command and Supervisory or
Instructor purposes.

b. All personnel assigned to "E" Squadron
or the 118th AAF Base Unit Bomb (M).

c. All personnel assigned to "C" Squadron,
except those officially designated for Command, Supervisory, or Instructor purposes.

5. Officers, Flight Officers and Warrant
Officer personnel undergoing OTU, Combat Crew
and Ground and Air Replacement Training will
not enter buildings or use tennis courts
listed in paragraph 3b, except on official
business and with prior approval of the Base
Commander, Deputy Base Commander, Director
for Administration and Services, Director for
Maintenance and Supply or Director of Operations and Training. After normal duty hours,
such approval will be obtained through the
Field Officer of the Day.

b. Base, Supervisory, Instructor or Command personal will not enter buildings or use tennis courts listed in paragraph 3a above except on official business and with prior approval of the Base Commander, Deputy Base Commander, Director of Administration and Services, director of Maintenance and Supply or Director for Operations and Training. After normal duty hours, such approval will be obtained through the Field Officer of the Day.

6. This order will be distributed to each officer presently assigned or assigned in the future to Freeman Field and will be read by each officer and returned to this Headquarters, certifying that he has read the order and that he fully understands it.

    BY ORDER COLONEL SELWAY

        (signed) DAVID H. THOMPSON

        Lt. Col., Air Corps

        Director for Maintenance and Supply

OFFICIAL

    (Signed) CHARLES J. McFARLANE

    Captain, Air Corps

    Asst. Adjutant

    1st Ind.

_____,Freeman Field, Seymour, Ind.

TO: Commanding Officer, Freeman Field, Seymour, Indiana.

I certify that I have read and fully understand the above order.

_____

Name

_____

Rank

_____

Organization

Appendix D: Arrestees

R-E-S-T-R-I-C-T-E-D

Headquarters
Freeman Field
Seymour, Indiana

SPECIAL ORDERS   12 April 1945
NUMBER 87

E-X-T-R-A-C-T

19. The following named officers, organizations indicated, will proceed on or about 13 April
1945 on temporary duty to Godman Field, Ky for
approximately ninety (90) days. Subject officers
are in arrest in quarters at Freeman Field Seymour
Ind and in arrest in transit from Freeman Field to
Godman Field Ky and upon arrival at Godman Field
are place in arrest in quarters at that station.
Orders for return to this station upon completion
of temporary duty will be issued by this headquarters. No per diem authorized while on this temporary duty.
TBMAA. CIPAP.   TDN 501-24 P 432-02 A 042525.

619th Bombardment Sq (M), 477th Bombardment Gp (M)
1ST LT ARTHUR L. WARD   0584177
1ST LT JAMES B. WILLIAMS   0867664
2ND LT DAVID A. SMITH   0585809
2ND LT WILLIAM C. PERKINS   01051725
2ND LT JAMES WHYTE JR.   0839096
2ND LT STEPHEN HOTESSE   02075599
2ND LT WARDELL A. POLK   0713064
2ND LT ROBERT E. LEE   02075548
2ND LT GEORGE H. KYDD   0828043
2ND LT DONALD D. HARRIS   02075544
F/O PAUL L. WHITE   T-136700
F/O CHARLES E. WILSON   T-62507
F/O JOHN E. WILSON   T-136703
F/O PAUL W. SCOTT   T-136685
F/O MC CRAY JENKINS   T-136661
F/O HARRIS H. ROBNETT   T-64629
F/O DONALD A. HAWKINS   T-67154
F/O GLEN W. PULLIAM   T-66410
F/O EUGENE L. WOODSON   T-136705

"E" Sq 118th AAF Base Unit (Bombardment - M)
2ND LT FRANK B. SANDERS   02080926
F/O WALTER M. MILLER   T-141234
F/O DENNY C. JEFFERSON   T-136714
F/O JAMES H. SHEPERD   T-64630
F/O EDWARD R. LUNDA   T-140111
2ND LT JAMES E. JONES   02075601
F/O SIDNEY H. MARZETTE   T-140114
2ND LT LEONARD A. ALTEMUS   02082572
F/O HOWARD STOREY T-136691
F/O JAMES C. WARREN   T-131958
2ND LT CLEOPHUS W. VALENTINE   0841276
F/O ARIO DIXIONE   T-140132
2ND LT ROBERT B. JOHNSON   02063893
F/O CALVIN SMITH   T-136687
F/O LEWIS C. HUBBARD JR.   T-136660
F/O WILLIAM J. CURTIS   T-68763
2ND LT CYRIL P. DYER   02080886
2ND LT VICTOR L. RANSON   02080924
F/O LLOYD W. GODFREY   T-138243
2ND LT COLEMAN A. YOUNG   01297128
2ND LT LE ROY F. GILLEAD   0713060
F/O CONNIE NAPPIER JR.   T-138250
2ND LT ARGONNE F. HARDEN   0841270
2ND LT ROBERT L. HUNTER   02082649
2ND LT JAMES W. BROWN JR.   0838186
2ND LT CHARLES E. DARNELL   0824824
2ND LT JAMES V. KENNEDY   0841271
2ND LT GLEN L. HEAD   02069201
F/O HARRY R. DICKENSON   T-140092
2ND LT QUENTIN P. SMITH   0841274
2ND LT CHARLES J. DORKINS   0841269
F/O MAURICE J. JACKSON JR.   T-140105
2ND LT HERDON M. CUMMINGS   0841277
2ND LT MITCHELL L. HIGGINBOTHAN   0841164
F/O ALFRED U. MC KENZIE   T-68765
2ND LT HERBERT J. SCHWING   0841273
F/O WENDELL G. FREELAND   T-141200
F/O DAVID J. MURPHY JR.   T-66406
2ND LT CLAVIN T. WARRICK   0841278
2ND LT ROBERT S. PAYTON JR.   01174673
2ND LT THEODORE O. MASON   0838167
F/O ADOLPHUS LEWIS JR.   T-140136
2ND LT LUTHER L. OLIVER   0841272
2ND LT EDWARD E. TILLMON   02080937
F/O FRANK V. PIVALO   T-136681

2ND LT LEONARD E. WILLIAMS 01054447
F/O NORMAN A. HOLMES T-141212
2ND LT ROY M. CHAPPELL 02068895
2ND LT LEROY A. BATTLE 02075525
F/O CHARLES E. MALONE T-138247
2ND LT WALTER R. RAY 02068902
F/O CHARLES R. TAYLOR T-136723
2ND LT ROGER PINES 02068901
F/O ROLAND A. WEBBER T-136695
2ND LT SAMUEL COLBERT 02082500
2ND LT RUDOLPH A. BERTHOUD 02082576
2ND LT CLIFFORD C. JARRETT 02075547
F/O MARCUS E. CLARKSON T-139615
2ND LT LE ROY H. FREEMAN 02080947
2ND LT GEORGE H. O. MARTIN 02068900
2ND LT MELVIN M. NELSON 02082653
2ND LT EDWARD W. WATKINS 08142096
F/O EDWARD R. TABBANOR T-131956
F/O CLARENCE C. CONWAY T-141193
F/O FREDRICK H. SAMUELS T-66149
2ND LT EDWARD V. HIPPS JR. 02068897
2ND LT EDWARD W. WOODWARD 02882639
F/O JOHN R. PERKINS JR. T-64270
F/O ALVIN B. STEELE T-140140
F/O HIRAM E. LITTLE T-140137
2ND LT GEORGE W. PRIOLEAU JR. 0713065
F/O MARCEL CLYNE T-131952
2ND LT ARTHUR O. FISHER 02080946
F/O CHARLES E. JONES T-140108
F/O CHARLES S. GOLDSBY T-68764
F/O WENDELL T. STOKES T-140123
2ND LT WILLIAM W. BOWIE JR. 02080867
F/O BERTRAM W. PITTS T-140119
2ND LT SILAS M. JENKINS 0838168
F/O HARRY S. LUM T-141228
F/O ROBERT T. MCDANIEL T-140697
F/O HAYDEL J. WHITE T-68712

        BY ORDER OF COLONEL SELWAY:

                         HERMAN A. TAPPER
                         Major, Air Corps,
                         Adjutant.

OFFICIAL:
        Herman A. Tapper,
        Major Air Corps,
        Adjutant.

Documentation

I was personally involved in the Freeman Field Mutiny. I was in the first group of 19 officers to enter the club. For my initial research, I called upon my personal files. However, the motivation that became the driving force behind my completing this story was the discovery of the huge amount of definitive information contained in the files at the Albert F. Simpson Historical Research Center at the Air University, Maxwell Air Force Base, Alabama. Most details come from this gold mine of information.

The document that I have used as a major source is "The Training of Negro Combat Units by the First Air Force." This document is in two volumes. The author was Capt. Earl D. Lyon, who had been assigned as historian for the First Bomber Command on January 12, 1944. Lyons had visited the 477th Bombardment Group at Godman Field twice; May 28 to June 2, 1944, and August 19 to 23, 1945. He found that during the disorder and reorganization of June 1945 routine staff visits were not permitted, and even courtesy visits were not encouraged. He believed that as a subject for general history, this Group, and the manner in which it was being handled, might become the most important subject in the command.

In Lyons' search for information, he received far less data than the amount requested. He interviewed members of the 477th Group that he felt were men of character, poise, and education, and received from these persons diametrically opposite descriptions of what went on in the Group. The official records proved to be of little value to Lyon, as this was considered white paper—a paper written from a white persepective. When he became aware of the disorder, the special study which he had been planning became a matter of greater exigency. He made a point of getting acquainted with the men in the Group, or men concerned with it. He collected paper. He had two concerns: accuracy to evaluate sources of unusually erratic reliability, and to be mindful of the lacunae—for almost all the sources were white.[74]

Included in these documents are direct transcripts of telephone conversations between First Air Force Headquarters, the 477th Bombardment Group Headquarters, and high officials at Headquarters Army Air Forces. The telephone transcripts and documents were collected by Lyon, and are chronologically arranged in Volume II.

In referring to these two volumes in the footnotes, the telephone conversations will be called "Telcon Vol. II," and information from Volume I will be referred to as "Training Vol. I."

The story of the Freeman Field mutiny has never been told in its entirety. It has only been told in bits and pieces, usually based on information from only one side of the story. Information germane to this story was classified for almost three decades, which prevented the complete story being told. Throughout these years there were vast gaps in the information that was available to the black officers, writers, and speakers. In order to tell this story they had to rely on hearsay, vague memories of individuals, and information supplied by a few whites. As a result, the accounts of this historic event exhibited many differences in the details. In some cases, the pertinent facts were changed or missing. In many instances, details of this mutiny had been added, subtracted, or omitted completely simply because the relevant information was classified and hidden. In these hidden files were complete transcripts of the recorded telephone conversations about this incident between commanders and high staff officers at all levels of command. These telephone conversations were unique. These recordings were not made surreptitiously, but as a matter of procedures understood and agreed to by all involved.

During this era, the making of a recording of a telephone conversation was not a simple task. Huge wire recording cylinders were used, and frequent changes of these cylinders were required during a long conversation. These recordings were then transcribed by secretaries or transcribers. Sometimes the sentence structure or grammar was not always the fault of the conversationalist, but due to the person transcribing the conversation. However, I have reported the actual transcribed telephone conversation as written, edited only lightly for ease of reading. The level of these conversations reach high into the ranks of the Army Air Forces. These include telephone conversations involving as high a level as the Deputy Commander of the Army Air Forces.

For many crucial events, using only excerpts from these telephone conversations would not suffice. To do so would risk leaving the reader with a fragmented understanding of the depth of resistance held by the First Air Force and Headquarters Army Air Force to the idea of a black bomber group. The detailed reporting of this group of telephone conversations was necessary to pull back the cloak of disguise of the real purposes of these commanders. These conversations were classified top secret for 28 years. However, in 1973, at the insistence of Col. Alan L. Gropman, the author of a magnificent story, *The Air Force Integrates*, these files were declassified. The Department of Defense to this day is very sensitive about this information, and Dr. Gropman— then Col. Gropman—had to fight a protracted battle with the Department to be able to use this information in a speech before the 1973 Tuskegee Airmen Convention in Washington, D.C.

During the years that these files remained classified, they were unavailable to journalists and historians, and even to those of us who were involved in the incident. Those of us who wanted to tell this story completely and accurately were forced to use records, opinions, and reports prepared by prejudiced military leaders and military historical officers. For instance, the official history of the 477th Bombardment Group does not mention this incident.

In addition to these telephone conversations, I turned to numerous newspaper articles written during the period by both the black and white press.

Footnotes

1. David Brinkley, *Washington Goes to War*, (New York, NY, A. A. Knopf: distributed by Random House, 1988), pp. 81-83

2. Bernard C. Nalty, *Strength for the Fight*, (New York, NY: The Free Press, A Division of Macmillan, Inc. 1986), p. 157

3. Interview with William "Bill" Ellis, Los Angeles, CA 1994

4. Charles E. Francis, *The Tuskegee Airmen*, (Boston, MA: Braden Publishing Co., 1988), p. 85

5. Nalty, *Strength for The Fight*, p. 1

6. Alan L. Gropman, *The Air Force Integrates*, 1945-1964 (Washington, DC, Office of Air Force History, 1978), p. 2

7. Gropman, *The Air Force Integrates*, p. 2

8. Interview with Lt. Col. (Ret) Alexander Jefferson, Honolulu, HI, March 1993

9. Gropman, *The Air Force Integrates*, p.2

10. TelconVol II, Gen. Giles and Gen. Hunter

11. J. Alfred Phelps, *Chappie, Life and Times of Daniel James, Jr.*, (Novato, CA: Presidio Press, 1991), p. 75

12. Capt. Earl D. Lyons, Training of Negro Combat Units by the First Air Force, Training Vol. I, Office Memorandum: Status of Freeman Field, dtd March 1, 1945, Albert F. Simpson Historical Research Center (AFSHRC) Maxwell Air Force Base, AL

13. Training Vol. I, Report of Racial Situation, Freeman Field, IN, March 31, 1945, p. 1

14. Training Vol. I, p. 184

15. Ibid.
16. Telcon Vol. II, Gen Hunter and Col. Selway
17. Nalty, *Strength for the Fight*, p. 136
18. Training Vol. I, p. 190
19. Ibid.
20. Telcon, Gen. Glenn and Col. Selway, April 6, 1945
21. Training Vol. I, p. 179
22. Telcon, Gen. Glenn and Col. Selway, April 6, 1945
23. Telcon, Gen. Hunter and Col. Selway, April 9, 1945
24. Ibid.
25. Ibid.
26. Personal file of military records of author
27. Training Vol. I, p. 235
28. Ibid.
29. Ibid.
30. Telcon Vol. II, Gen. Glenn and Col. Selway
31. Telcon Vol. II, Gen. Kuter and Gen. Hunter, April 10, 1945
32. Telcon Vol. II, Gen. Owens and Gen. Hunter, April 11, 1945
33. Telcon Vol. II, Gen. Hunter and Col. Selway, April 12, 1945
34. National Archives Record Group AG 291.2, July 27, 1945, hereafter referred to as NARG AG 291.2
35. Telcon Vol. II, Gen. Hunter and Col. Selway, April 12, 1945
36. Telcon Vol. II, Gen. Kuter and Gen. Hunter, April 12, 1945
37. Telcon Vol. II, Gen. Kuter, Gen. Owens and Gen. Hunter, April 12, 1945
38. Telcon Vol. II, Gen. Hunter and Col. Selway, 1500 April 12, 1945
39. NARG AG 291.2, April 11, 1945
40. NARG ACOB-C 291.2, April 11, 1945
41. NARG AG 291.2, April 10, 1945
42. Francis, *The Tuskegee Airmen*, pp. 206-207
43. Training Vol. I, Letter Gen. Hunter to Col. Selway, Subject: Security, dated April 20, 1945
44. Col. Selway's first endorsement to Gen Hunter's letter of April 20, 1945
45. Personal interview with Mr. William "Bill" Ellis, at Tuskegee Airman Annual Convention in Boston, MA, August 1992
46. Telcon Vol. II, Gen. Hunter and Col. Selway, April 14, 1945
47. Telcon Gen Owens and Gen. Hunter, April 14, 1945
48. Telcon Vol. II, Gen. Hunter and Gen. Hedrick, April 16, 1945
49. Training Vol. I, p. 115
50. NARG AG WDCSO 291.2 Negroes, June 7, 1945 Memorandum for the Honorable John J. McCloy, Chairman, Advisory Committee on Special Troop Policies, May 31, 1945
51. Ibid. These remarks and recommendations on the Proposed Report of Advisory Committee Meeting stating the Army Air Forces position were written by Brig. Gen. Ray L. Owens, Deputy Chief of the Air Staff

52. NARG SPAP 291.2 June 2, 1945
53. Major General W.H. Edwards, memorandum for Lt. Col. Jones, Subject: Change in War Department Pamphlet 20-6
54. Telcon Vol. II, Gen. Owens and Gen. Glenn, May 10, 1945
55. NARG AG SPAP 291. 2 Memorandum for the Secretary of War from John J. McCloy, Subject: Report of Advisory Committee on Special Troop Policies, June 4, 1945
56. Telcon Vol II, Gen Welsh and Col. Stewart, April 18, 1945
57. Gropman, *The Air Force Integrates*, p. 272
58. Material referencing the *Fortune* article was taken from an editorial printed in the *Chicago Defender*, "Is the Negro Press Inflammatory?" dated May 5, 1945
59. Telcon Vol. II, Gen. Hunter and Col. Haddock, April 26, 1945
60. Telcon Vol. II, Gen Hunter and Col. Selway, April 24, 1945
61. Telcon Vol. II, Gen. Giles and Gen. Hunter, April 23, 1945
62. Francis, *The Tuskegee Airmen*, p. 208
63. Ibid.
64. Telcon Vol. II, Gen. Born and Gen. Glenn
65. Telcon Vol. II, Gen. Glenn and Col. Urbach, April 20, 1945
66. Telcon Vol. II, Gen. Anderson and Gen. Glenn, June 29, 1945
67. Telcon Vol. II, Gen. Hunter and Col. Kirksey, June 29, 1945
68. Telcon Vol. II, Gen. Glenn and Col. Davis, June 30, 1945
69. The details of the trial are from the Court-Martial Records of these two trials. Department of the Army Judiciary, NASSIF Building, Fall Church, VA
70. Lawrence P. Scott and William M. Womack, Sr., *Double V, The Civil Rights Struggle of the Tuskegee Airmen* (East Lansing, MI, Michigan State University Press), p. 244
71. Phelps, *Chappie, Life and Times of Daniel James, Jr.*, p. 158
72. Benjamin O. Davis, Jr., *An Autobiography, Benjamin O. Davis, Jr. :American* (Washington, D C: Smithsonian Institution Press) p. 145
73. Training Vol. I, p. 31
74. Telephone conversation with Dr. Alan Gropman, 1994

The Final Chapter

Shortly after publication of this book, the Air Force chose to exonerate all airmen who had participated in the Freeman Field Mutiny. During the 1995 Annual Convention of Tuskegee Airmen, exactly 50 years after the mutiny, the Air Force made its formal announcement.

All of us who had been victimized by the original action were heartened by this present-day, enlightened response, I cannot speak for all the others who were finally vindicated by the Air Force decision, but I have an idea that their experiences, their feelings, and their reactions during the years after the mutiny were much like mine.

After I had been recalled to active duty for the Korean War, and had completed my tour of duty in Korea, I elected to continue service in the United States Air Force. I wanted an Air Force career even though I knew I had a time bomb ticking in my records, namely the reprimand that I had received on April 24, 1945, for my participation in the Freeman Field incident.

The Air Force had been separated from the Army in 1948, President Truman had ended segregation in the military with Executive Order 9981, and it was my hope that in the modern, integrated Air Force this reprimand would be evaluated in light of the inflexible segregation in place in the armed forces during World War Two. I believed my reprimand would not limit my progress toward a successful Air Force career, rather that it would be put in proper perspective when I was under consideration for acceptance into senior military schools necessary for advancement and promotion.

When I realized I was not being selected for schools, or getting assignments I felt I had earned, my superior performance notwithstanding, I concluded that the reprimand must still have been an important consideration. The words extracted from and attached to my record, "He displayed an uncooperative and stubborn attitude toward constituted authority," were having a devastating affect on my career.

I looked at the justification required for a successful petition to the Board of Corrections of Military Records, and realized I would need overwhelming proof that an injustice had been done before I could petition the Board to remove my reprimand. I was unable to find necessary proof during my active career, and retired in 1978 as a lieutenant colonel.

I never gave up on my dream of removing the reprimand. When I read Alan Gropman's book, *The Air Force Integrates*, and learned of the documents he had found, I was encouraged. I thought here was a source that should supply me with sufficient material to convince the Board. After researching the documents, I was convinced that the information would not only be sufficient for my personal request, but allow me an attempt to reach another of my dreams, that of telling the story of the Freeman Field mutiny completely and accurately, something that had never been done. This book is the fulfillment of that dream.

Another almost incredible result to this story has occurred. With the information I had gathered, I telephoned D. Michael Collins, Deputy for Equal Opportunity in the office of Rodney A. Coleman, Assistant Secretary of the Air Force, and asked for assistance in submitting a request for the correction of military records. In that request I asked that the Board for Corrections remove the reprimand not merely from my record, but from the records of all 100 other officers who had received it, as well. In addition, I requested that the Board consider setting aside the conviction of Lt. Roger C. Terry as unjust.

The following is the news release of Aug. 12, 1995, from the Air Force News Service in its entirety:

Air Force removes stain from Tuskegee Airmen's records

ATLANTA — Retired Air Force Lt. Col. James C. Warren and 100 other black Army Air Force officers stood against an unlawful order at Freeman Field, Ind., in 1945 and each received a letter of reprimand for his actions.

The men had tried to enter the base officers club, which had been integrated by War Department policy, but again segregated by the local commander.

Fifty years later, on Aug. 12 in Atlanta, the Air Force vindicated Warren and 14 other Tuskegee Airmen members by removing the letters of reprimand from their permanent military records. The letter was one of the strongest administrative actions a commander could impose on a service member.

Rodney A. Coleman, assistant secretary of the Air Force for manpower, reserve affairs, installations and environment, announced the Air Force decision during the Tuskegee Airmen annual banquet.

He also announced that the Air Force had set aside a court-martial conviction against another former Army Air Force officer, Roger C. Terry, who is president of the Tuskegee Airmen, Inc. Additionally, the service restored all the rights, privileges and property Terry had lost because of the conviction.

Air Force Chief of Staff Gen. Ronald R. Fogleman, who was the banquet's guest speaker, presented the official documents to Warren and Terry.

"With this action, a terrible wrong in the annals of U.S. Air Force and U. S . military history has been righted," said Coleman. He said the Air Force will remove the letters of reprimand from the other 89 former officer's records as soon as it receives their requests.

Earlier in his remarks, Coleman called the Freeman Field incident a "bellwether for change with respect to integrating the U.S. military." He said the men who took part in the actions had taken "a giant step for equality" nine years before Rosa Parks refused to sit in the back of the bus in Montgomery, Ala., and paved the way for changes "in the soon-to-be brand-new service—the U.S. Air Force."

Warren, who had been a flight officer in training at Freeman Field, started the letter removal process by writing to Coleman and asking the Air Force to consider correcting the records of everyone involved in the Freeman Field incident.

Coleman said his office worked with the records correction board to investigate the circumstances of the 50-year-old incident, which Warren describes in his book, "The Freeman Field Mutiny."

"The 104 officers involved in the so-called 'mutiny' have lived the last 50 years knowing they were right in what they did—yet feeling the stigma of an unfair stain on their records because they were fighting men, too—and wanted to be treated as such," said Coleman.

The Freeman Field incident began April 1, 1945, when the base commander issued a letter segregating trainees from base and supervisory officers. At the time, all the trainees were black, and all base and supervisory personnel were white, said Coleman.

"The actual effect of the letter was to segregate the officers clubs on the basis of race, and authorized discrimination in violation of War Department policy," said Coleman.

Four days after posting the letter, the commander heard that some newly-arriving black officers would try to enter the club, so he ordered all doors locked except the main entrance. He then posted military police at the club to keep out all "non-members."

That night, April 5, 1945, numerous groups of black officers tried to enter the club, Coleman said. Terry, who was a second lieutenant, brushed against a superior officer to gain entrance and was subsequently charged and convicted by general court-martial of assault. Two other officers were also court-martialed, but later acquitted of all charges, said Coleman.

Those given letters of reprimand were charged with "conduct unbecoming an officer, failure to obey a lawful order, and breach of good order and discipline."

Normally, requests to correct military records must be filed within three years of an incident. However, in this case, the Air force waived that ruling.

Other officers whose records have already been corrected are: James B. Williams, James W. Whyte Jr., Alvin B. Steele, Frederick H. Samuels, Wardell A. Polk, Charles E. Malone, Edward R. Lunda, Adolphus Lewis Jr., James V. Kennedy, Edward V. Hipps, Mitchell L. Higginbotham, Lloyd W. Godfrey, and Roy M. Chappell.

The Tuskegee Airmen Convention

Atlanta, Georgia, August 12, 1995

5

6

1. USAF Chief of Staff Gen. Ronald R. Fogelman, Roger Terry, and Assistant Secretary of the Air Force Rodney C. Coleman, at the moment of announcement. **2**. D. Michael Collins, Deputy for Equal Opportunity in the office of Rodney Coleman. **3**. Oliver Goodall, one of the first officers to enter the club at Freeman Field. **4**. Adolphus Lewis, Jr., just after the official announcement. **5**. Walter Kyle at the HBO movie, *The Tuskegee Airmen,* written by Robert Williams, and premiered at the convention. **6**. Ed Woodward and his wife, Lee. **7**. Author James C. Warren and his wife, Xanthia. *(Photos by Donna Ewald.)*

7

Index